LAW COLLOQUY JOURNAL OF LEGAL STUDIES, VOLUME - I, ISSUE - III

LAW COLLOQUY

Copyright © Law Colloquy
All Rights Reserved.

DEDICATED TO
ALMIGHTY

Contents

ABOUT ORGANISATION

LAW COLLOQUY

'**Law Colloquy**' has been created for documenting short precise and substantive **articles/ notes/ videos/ news** on perceptions regarding various important topics of law. We aim to make people familiar with the different **theories, statutes, laws,** and to help one understand and develop the legal mindset. We also conduct **Webinars/Seminars/workshops/conferences and training programs** on different aspects of the law for different target groups.

Law Colloquy's mission is to provide a common platform for **academicians, professionals, students, researchers,** and **scholars** to discuss key issues and developments in the area of **corporate, company, banking, politics, law, management, economics, and social sciences** by participating in **international academic conferences, seminars, webinars, and workshops.**

www.lawcolloquy.com

Message From Director's Desk

Dear **Readers,**

We are delighted to announce the release of **Law Colloquy Journal of Legal Studies (LCJLS) Volume 1 Issue 3.** Law Colloquy has **LCJLS** is a peer-reviewed journal, built to incorporate and motivate research on diverse areas of law based on analyzing legal and contemporary issues, policy decisions, case studies, proposing/recommending legislative reforms, or judgment analysis.

The **LCJLS** is a quarterly journal. **Law Colloquy** has formulated a set pattern of citation and reference. We encourage to use of **Harvard** (in text) referencing style which is widely implemented and acceptable in various international journals. **Author(s)/Contributors** are required to follow this pattern.

This issue is really special for all of us because this year **Law Colloquy** organized our first **Virtual International Conference on Crime and Criminal Justice System (ICCCJS).** We have incorporated the selected scholarly research papers from the conference proceeding.

We are overwhelmed to have such a tremendous response from scholars of the entire world. I extend my sincere thanks to the esteemed board members for their continued support and guidance. I appreciate the earnest efforts of our editorial team who worked very hard.

Once again I heartily thank all **scholars, academicians, and students** for their sincere contribution.

We look forward to more contributions in the future.

Happy reading!

Prof. (Dr) Priya Sepaha

Founder Director, Editor In Chief & Publisher

Email: directorlawcolloquy@gmail.com

I

Regulation of Telecommunications Industry in India

Authored By: Ashwin Gupta
Student Amity Law School, Noida

· **Abstract**

Reforms have enabled the telecoms industry to handle a wide array of concerns such as service quality, consumer interest protection, and the rise of rural communications services. Furthermore, both the regulatory process and the court are significant determinants for attracting investment, and its success has triggered a phenomenal rise in wired and wireless telephony and added value services. India has to be on its current road to change to benefit the telecoms sector and its customers from new technology.

This paper examines the Indian telecom sector's transition from a monopolistic to a competitive environment. Even though similar transitions have occurred in other countries, India's shift is particularly notable due to the rapidity with which changes occurred. The National Telecommunications Policy, 1994, and the New Telecommunications Policy, 1999 established a strong and independent regulatory mechanism with well-defined powers and responsibilities. By setting service provider criteria, verifying compliance, and developing a structure for dispute resolution, this regulatory mechanism helps maintain a competitive environment in the services sector.

· **Key Words**: *telecom, law, regulations, reforms*

· **Introduction**

The paradigm shift in the Indian telecommunications market had followed the pattern observed elsewhere in the framework of deregulation of that sector from the monopoly system to one of open competitiveness(duopoly) and the subsequent development of an independent telecom regulatory system. The Government of India (G.O.I.) had adopted and implemented policy measures that take account of the ground conditions. With the advent of private players in the 1980s, the reform process began.into the manufacturing of customer premise equipment in 1984, the corporatization of domestic telecom operations in two metropolises: Delhi and Mumbai, and the formation of an international services corporation in 1986 and a Telecom Commission with full government powers in 1989.(Prasad, 2008). Although the incremental reforms implemented in the 1980s were steps toward freeing bureaucratic control, they had a monopolistic tone.

The declaration of an economic liberalization agenda by the Government of India in 1991 gave the virtual drive for transformation. This strategy indicated a shift in policy makers' attitudes, which resulted in a structural transformation in the Indian economy (Venkatnarayana,2015). Policymakers were acutely aware of the need to boost the infrastructure sector, which served as the economy's backbone. The choice of the telecom sector to "showcase" the policy shift underlined the Government's importance of telecommunications as an ordinaryperson's tool for capacity building, a significant driver of economic and social transformation, and a factor in developing the country's international competitiveness.

· **Past Constraints**

Before liberalization, India's telecommunications market was in shambles. The government monopoly was characterized by abysmally low teledensity, weak tele-infrastructure, a limited-service portfolio, and a highly bureaucratized structure. The NTP94 estimated that the teledensity was around 0.8 per hundred people, compared to a global average of 10 per hundred people, and that it was considerably lower in several developing nations (Kathuria, 2004). The policy document admitted around eight million lines in the network with a waiting list of about 2.5 million and tele-coverage of nearly 140,000 villages out of 576,490 communities, highlighting the poor situation in tele-infrastructure(Subramaniam,2008).The position in India then was poorer than in many developing countries, including many low-income countries. Furthermore, the fixed-line service tariff remained highly high—local, S.T.D., and I.S.D.Per-minute call prices (in INR) were 16.80, 30.00, and 75.00 respectively in 1997 but had dropped to 1.0, 2.4, and 6.40 in 2007.

The Government was aware of the imperatives of enhancing and modernizing telecommunication infrastructure in terms of volume, accessibility, and cost, having acknowledged telecommunications's impact on people's lives and the country. There, the G.O.I. also acknowledged telecoms' catalytic role in other countries' development processes, as well as global changes in the telecom landscape caused by increasing globalization, technological advancements, rapidly growing consumer needs, and new demands emerging from the unleashing of market forces.

· **National Telecom Policy, 1994**

Giving effect to this conclusion and successfully liberalizing requires large amounts of investment and structural changes in the telecom behemoth. This could have been the start of a new policy endeavour that resulted in the National Telecom Policy 1994 (Kokil,2007). This policy statement was the first attempt in India to formalize policy objectives and give a roadmap for telecom development. Specific targets were included in the strategy statement, such as making telephone service available on-demand, covering all villages, providing PCOs in urban areas for every 500 people by 1997, and introducing all value-added services available worldwide, preferably by 1996. The expected resource deficit for achieving these aims was considerably over Rs.230 billion. Hence the strategy stressed private sector involvement and the need for private investment to bridge the resource gap.

As a result, for the first time, the policy authorized private enterprises registered in India to supplyessential telephone services under certain conditions. It instituted a duopoly regime with two operators in each of the four metros and eighteen telecom circles. Another significant aspect of this policy paper was its emphasis on safeguarding and promoting consumer interests, as well as ensuring fair competition. Although the NTP94 did not go far enough in terms of liberalization, it did remove the umbilical cord that had been binding the Indian telecom sector to its monopoly provider, which had been nurtured by the more-than-a-century-old Indian Telegraph Act (Kathuria, 2019). However, the policy's implementation fell short of the excitement it generated, yielding mixed effects. Physical targets, notably for rural telephones, were not met. By March 1999, only approximately half of the over 600,000 communities had been covered (Johnson, 2012).

The NTP94 placed a high priority on safeguarding consumer interests and promoting fair competition. The Telecom Regulatory Authority of India Act 1997 was enacted by the Government in 1997, resulting in the establishment of an independent statutory Regulatory Authority for the telecom sector, with clearly defined functions, powers, and responsibilities to encourage competition, ensure a level playing field, and promote and protect consumer interests. The Telecom Regulatory Authority of India (TRAI) has broad functions and powers in the sectors under its jurisdiction. These include ensuring technical compatibility and effective interconnection between operators and serviceproviders,regulating revenue-sharing agreements between service providers, monitoring quality-of-service standards, ensuring compliance with license conditions, approving telecom tariffs, and protecting consumer interests (Garg, 2020). The Telecom Regulator was not tasked with tasks such as licensing, standard formulation, and spectrum allocation, which fall under the purview of the Government.

- **New Telecom Policy, 1999**

While the execution of NTP94 did have a considerable effect, it was deemed inadequate in resolving competition issues. Many projects encountered difficulties for two main reasons: first, actual revenues realized fell well short of predictions; and second, operators were unable to secure funding for their projects. The enunciation of a New Telecom Policy 1999 was a response to the profound changes occurring in the telecom sector worldwide, as well as the shortcomings of NTP94. The NTP99 broadened the scope of cellular mobile service, fixed service, cable service, and license terms and conditions and operational features. Interconnection had been a significant source of contention among service providers and had resulted in numerous disagreements. Recognizing the severity of the issue, the Government incorporated it into policy in NTP99. The NTP99 policy stated explicitly that interconnection between service providers in the mobile and primary service sectors was permitted.

1. Establishment of a Telecom Dispute Resolution and Appellate Tribunal

In 2000, a modification to the TRAI Act separated the regulatory and adjudicatory roles by creating a specialized statutory dispute settlement system, the Telecom Disputes Settlement and Appellate Tribunal (TDSAT).Subject to certain restrictions, this body's functions include adjudicating any conflict between a licensor and a licensee, two or more service providers, or a service provider. A group of consumers has the authority to control its proceedings and has both original and appellate jurisdictions. The civil court delegated jurisdiction to TDSAT on subjects within the latter's competence, and the latter's orders are executable as a civil court decree. On legal grounds, the Supreme Court of India may hear an appeal against the TDSAT's orders (Srivastava, 2016).

2. Convergence of Markets and Technologies

The Communication Convergence Bill of 2001 made considerable headway in shaping this trend. Despite being introduced in Parliament, this Bill made little progress and expired before becoming law (Patnaik, 2002). Broadcasting and cable services were eventually included in the term "telecommunication service" as defined in the TRAI Act, 1997, and revised in 2000 by a government notification dated January 9, 2004. As a result, the telecomregulator had jurisdictionover broadcasting and cable services, and disputes resulting from these services were within the telecom sector's appellate body (Maheshwari, 2020).

3. Infrastructure Sharing

Previously, passive infrastructure sharing was permitted, allowing a new telecom operator to rent space on another's tower to place its equipment to support its rollout. With the new rule on active infrastructure sharing, a new entrant can now rent all active electronics, switches, and circuits from another telecom operator who possesses passive and active infrastructure. However, active infrastructure sharing does not include spectrum sharing. This rule will assist new operators in launching their services with less upfront capital investment, resulting in increased viability and cheaper rates. The cheaper cost of providing service will encourage service providers to expand telecom services in rural areas without incurring the substantial costs of telecom coverage in such places.

- **Influence of Regulatory Efforts**

1. ***Telecom Regulator and Dispute Resolution Entity as a stimulus for telecommunication development***

The independent regulator had established itself as a fixture in the telecom sector, and the depth of its dedication to serving as an umpire for the industry instilled confidence in both customers and service providers. The regulator and the dispute resolution agency had both matured into credible institutions, which was well for the telecom sector. The influence of the telecom regulator's activities spanning several facets of telecom services had been beneficial to expanding the telecom sector. Similarly, the TDSAT dispute resolution mechanism provided an excellent platform for focused issue resolution, and the consistency of its approach had significantly increased investor confidence(Prasad, 2007).

The telecom regulator faced enormous problems following deregulation, as it was expected to address a slew of concerns in areas like rate setting, quality of service, consumer protection, licensing, rural telecom service growth, and spectrum management. Dealing with these difficulties properly through legislation and integrating stakeholders in the process was critical to ensuring a level playing field, stimulating competitiveness, and increasing customer happiness. The regulator fully addressed these challenges, resulting in the telecom sector's revolution in India.

2. ***Tariffs***

The Telecom Regulatory Authority of India recognized the importance of an inexpensive rate for the average person as a stimulant for much-needed telecom network expansion and as a toolfor boostingcompetition in the sector early on. Increased competition in the telecom sector has given service providers the freedom to provide whatever rate they want as long as they meet specific regulatory guidelines,such as I.U.C.(Interconnect Usage Charges) compliance (Mathews,2011). The first significant policy step was the 1999 Telecommunications Tariff Order (T.T.O.), in which the tariff structure of various telecom services had become transparent. This T.T.O. also conveyed signals to potential investors in the sector regarding the way telecom price reforms are being conducted, the main factors being:

- Further rebalancing prices to match with expenses while focusing on the social goal of encouraging non-users of telecom to connect to the system and utilize it more intensely;
- Enhanced flexibility for pricing and consumer choice for service providers.

3. *Quality of Services(QoS)*

In July 2000, the regulator established regulations on Q.O.S. for essential and cellular services, with different parameters supplied for wireline and wireless services, in compliance with its duty to define guidelines for the quality of service provided by various service providers. The TRAI has been reviewing the status of the quality of service supplied by operators regularly. The overall performance of wireline services in comparison to the benchmarks was determined to be poor in these studies. In the case of mobile service providers, however, they discovered that overall performance was far better, with almost 75% of the operators meeting most of their benchmarks. The TRAI classified basic and cellular Q.O.S. metrics into four areas under this regulation (Ardagna, 2014):

- Network performance;
- Customer helplines;
- Billing complaints; and
- Customer impression of services.

4. *Protecting of Consumer Services*

The TRAI has addressed consumers' concerns in a variety of ways, including:

- Holding half-yearly meetings with registered consumer organizations to gain a better understanding of their problems;
- Inviting consumer organizations to seminars, workshops, and conferences to inform them of various developments in the telecom sector; and

- Prescribing a written voluntary declaration by the consumer organizations

All of these steps increased consumers' impressions of the efficacy of telecom services and served as a warning to service providers that they must conform to the regulator's standards or face the consequences. These pro-consumer policies aided telecom expansion in India, as seen by the welcome increase in teledensity in both urban and rural areas

5. *Provision of tele-connectivity in Rural Areas*

The significant disparity between rural and urban teledensity has long necessitated immediate response. In the third quarter of 2007, the rural wireline customer count added up to 11.99 million. Both the NTP94 and the NTP99 stressed the importance of expanding rural tele-coverage. The number of village public telephones (V.P.T.) has consistently increased over the years, rising from 0.68 per 100 in 1999-2000 to 8.35 in December 2007 (Majumbar,2020).According to the Annual Report of the Department of Telecommunications,2007-08, about 527,000 VPTs in the country are currently eligible for financial assistance for operation and maintenance through the USOF (Universal Service Obligation Fund) (Malakar, 2015)

6. *Spectrum Management*

The NTP99 acknowledged that the continuous proliferation of new technologies, together with rising demand for telecom services, has resulted in a plethora of spectrum demands. As a result, the policy emphasized the importance of efficient, logical exploitation of this precious resource, as well as the importance of transparency in the process of allocating frequency spectrum. The availability and efficient use of spectrum were critical components in increasing service quality, growing the network, and successfully shifting to an era of service and technology convergence (Majumbar,2020). Some of the crucial issues that were relevant in this context were as follows:

- Should the number of access providers be limited?
- Should the allocation of spectrum be accompanied by constraints for its use, such as adherence to a timetable and/or compliance with rollout

responsibilities associated with previously given spectrum?
- What metrics should be used to calculate spectrum pricing?
- Should the spectrum-allocation strategy be flexible and independent of any single technology, letting service providers select its use?

The proposals of the TRAI centre on providing a level playing field, establishing technological neutrality, and assuring affordability. It had also suggested that in the future, after reserving the spectrum in particular bands, the spectrum be allocated through auctions. Since there was insufficient spectrum to meet the needs of existing operators, let alone new applicants, an efficient, equitable method is clearly in the best interests of the telecom industry (Ardagna, 2014).

- **Future Challenges**

The fundamental difficulty confronting India's telecom sector is the importance of telecommunication infrastructure in a country's economic and social life. How the telecom sector responds to that challenge is determined by two factors: first, how it addresses the concerns and needs of all segments of Indian society, and second, how it uses current technologies (and assimilates new technologies) to reduce internal barriers to Indian development and improve India's ability to compete globally. The Indian telecommunications industry has come a long way, but it still has a long way to go. To finish the journey efficiently, the industry must critically assess the extent to which policy objectives have been met, identify and fix areas where current policies are lacking, and forecast what new policies will be required to adapt to developing conditions (Maheshwari, 2020).

Another significant difficulty would be to reconsider the roles of the regulator and the dispute resolution institution as the telecom industry matures. The industry is distinguished by increasing network complexity, market segmentation into outlying areas and niches that serve diverse clients, and the heightened importance of technical breakthroughs in driving change. Regulatory bodies will increasingly be called upon to address difficulties arising from cross-platform competition. The needs of a fast-expanding and changing business will raise concerns regarding the suitable form of its regulating body. What powers, functions, and responsibilities should the regulator be given, and how should it be staffed to carry them out? Furthermore, how should its independence and protection from external meddling be ensured? Similar problems exist concerning the dispute-resolution institution, which will also need to prepare itself to deal with new forms of disputes promptly.

Finally, issues emerge from the need to increase teledensity and lay the groundwork for introducing new technology and services. Protocols for third- and fourth-generation networks must also be developed by authorities. In addition, developing and executing a sound, transparent spectrum policy will remain a principal focus.

· Closing Arguments

The promotion of a competitive environment in the service industry, such as telecom, is mainly dependent on an independent, powerful regulatory apparatus based on status conveying specified powers, functions, and responsibilities. The regulator is enabled by this framework to operate transparently and to lay down ground rules, and then monitor service providers' conformity with them. An effective conflict resolution procedure, which objectively and promptly resolves disagreements, is also necessary for a competitive setting. To implement the dramatic changes arising from convergence, business changes to practice and growing consumer expectations in the telecommunications sector, the quality and transparency of regulation and the efficacy of the dispute settlement process remain essential aspects to attract investment. The political organization contributes equally to the clarity and transparency of the political system and the positive assistance of the regulatory institutions. If any vital agency fails to fulfil its particular tasks successfully, the reform process will be affected.

The telecommunications industry in India has travelled a long way and emerged from its early efforts to develop the core service into the current period of amazing landline and cellular telephony growth and value-added services. The sector has overcome numerous challenges to its current development phase but has to continue to reform if new technologies fulfil their promise and become an engine of equitable economic development.

· References

1. Anonymous, Sharing Networks Driving Growth- I.T.U. News Magazine (2006),   https://www.itu.int/en/itunews/Documents/2017/2017-06/

2017_ITUNews06-en.pdf

2. Anonymous, Telecom Sector Reforms in India- Cellular Operators Association of India(Nov. 2007), https://cdn.coai.com/sites/default/files/2017-04/White-Paper-Telecom-Reforms-in-India-

3. Rajat Kathuria, One Step Forward Two-Step Backwards- LIVEMINT (November 12, 2019), https://www.livemint.com/opinion/columns/one-step-forward-two-steps-back-for-telecom-sector-11573575502560.htmlNov.2007.pdfhttps://scholarworks.lib.csusb.edu/cgi/viewcontent.cgi?article=1072&context=ciima

4. Anonymous, TRAI announces service rules for D.T.H. and Telecom Companies- Economic Times (August 31, 2007), https://economictimes.indiatimes.com/industry/telecom/trai-announces-quality-of-service-rules-for-dth/articleshow/2327206.cms?from=mdr

5. D. Ardagna, Quality-of-service in cloud computing- Journal of Internet Services and Applications (Sep. 2014), https://jisajournal.springeropen.com/articles/10.1186/s13174-014-0011-3

6. Department of Telecommunications, Telecom Regulatory Authority of India(Amendment) Act, 2000, https://www.trai.gov.in/sites/default/files/The_TRAI_(Amendment)_Act_2000.pdf

7. KapouMalakar, A Situational Analysis of the Impact of Liberalism on Policy Paradigm and Growth Stats of Telecommunication in India- International Journal of English Language, Literature and Humanities, Vol. 3 Issue 1 (2015), http://ijellh.com/wp-content/uploads/2015/04/38._Kapou-malakar.pdf

8. Medha Srivastava, The TDSAT Revisited- VIDHI Centre for Legal Policy (Jun. 2016), https://tdsat.gov.in/admin/notice/uploads/TDSAT%20Vidhi%206%20june%202016.pdf

II

Freedom of Trade and Commerce – A Constitutional View Point

Authored By: Sandhya Prabhakaran
Amity Law School, Noida

· **Abstract**

Trade and commerce have become the largest sectors through which countries develop. Be it already developed countries like Japan or the USA or developing countries like India, trade and commerce has been the root of the survival of the world since ancient times. Evolution, development, and urbanization led to the rapid growth of the human race. Education has become a significant part of countries, and with the need for development came the need for laws. The need for constitutional law travels way back o 1215 when Magna Carta became the most important process that led to constitutional law in today's nations. Countries developed while enacting multiple laws for the protection of their respective citizens. Today with more than 190 countries globally, 167 out of them being democratic, constitutional law has gone through multiple changes and amendments. As far as the Indian Constitution is concerned, it was amended 105 times as per August

2021 data. India provides six primary fundamental rights to its citizens, explained in detail under Part III of the Constitution. Out of the six, one primary fundamental right that falls under the right to freedom is the Freedom of Trade and Commerce. It is widely explained under Sub-clause (g) of clause (1) of Article 19.

Moreover, provisions for freedom of trade, commerce, and intercourse are also separately explained under part XIII of the Constitution – Articles 301 to 307.One of the fundamental rights granted to citizens is the freedom of trade and commerce. More than 40% of India's population is involved in trade and commerce. Every citizen has the right to work in the occupation of their choosing.; they can freely profess and practice any profession, occupation of their choice throughout the territory of India. This right is not absolute and does have some exceptions. The Parliament can impose certain restrictions on this right for the public interest. For example, if a particular business is not legal, then the government has the right to stop the persons involved in such business from carrying it on any further. This will not mean that their right to practice and profess any occupation of choice freely is violated. It must be noted that freedom does not make one free from laws. This paper explains the constitutional provisions related to freedom of trade and commerce in detail.

- ***Keywords***: *Freedom of Trade and Commerce, Magna Carta, Part III of the Constitution, Article 19 (1) (g), Part XIII of the Constitution, Articles 301 – 307, Fundamental Rights.*

- **Introduction –**

The Constitution of India can into force on January 26th 1950, making India a Republic. The Indian Constitution is the world's most extensive Constitution and is a written constitution. It provides the various rules, regulations, principles, rights, and duties for governing the organs of the Government of a State. It is a fact that the Constitution of India has gone through eminent research and deliberations for the improvement of the administration system. India's Constitution establishes fundamental rights and responsibilities for its inhabitants. One of them is the Freedom of Trade and Commerce that is explained in detail in this paper.

The Constitution's Article 19 (1) (g) guarantees the right to practice any profession. It explains that every citizen of the country can freely practice any profession and trade or business of their choice. Part XIII of the Constitution widely discussed trade, commerce, and intercourse within the territory of India. Articles 301 to 307 fall under this part.

It is a good fact that India is neither wholly a federal-state nor unitary; it is called quasi-federal. By quasi-federal, it must be inferred that there are two sets of government – the central government and the state governments, where more power is given to the central government. Here, it is significant to note that the Centre is not dominating the State, but relatively few provisions can be handled only by the Centre. For example, a situation of national emergency, even in one part of any State cannot be declared by the Governor, only the honourable President of India can declare a situation to be of national emergency if he is satisfied that such situation is making the parts of the State or the State or any part of the nation lose its peace.

In all federations, the nation is deemed to create, preserve, and develop the economy by removing the barriers to domestic economic activities and induce trade and commerce for making the nation one single economic unit for the common advantage of everyone [1].

As far as the Indian Constitution is concerned, the framers felt the significance to maintain the significance of economic unity of the nation. India has been famous for trade since the subcontinent era and is known to have good relations throughout the silk routes of the country. India was one of the largest economies of the world before the British era. Punch marked trade coins, muslin cloths, spices, and many more trade items were exported from India. It is evident throughout the history of India that trade has been in the blood, and traders exported products of variety across the globe.

Maritime trade happened between the Southern Part of India and Southeast and West Asia from the early 14th Century CE. Back in the time, Malabar Coast and Coromandel Coast were important locations of trade centers. During the Maurya era, faster infrastructural developments such as the building of roads were improvised that gave traders to find out various routes of trade. Along with the building of warehouses, the profession of trading started to grow at a faster pace, and traders felt security with these developments.

India's trade routes grew, and many scholars provided suggestions to improvise trade relations with Eastern Europe. Many traders settled in India between 14th and 18th centuries. This became a boom period for Commerce in India. Towards the north, the Bengal and Saurashtra coasts were significant contributors to maritime trade. The Gangetic Plains, Indus Valley, Punjab region all contributed to trade and commerce with agricultural produces.

The period of the Delhi Sultanate made India develop international trade relations that included social and economic relations. The Sultanate era brought in mechanical technologies, and India adopted them widely.

· **Historical Background –**

Agriculture is regarded as India's economic backbone, and more than 50% of the GDP contributions is by the agriculture sector. India has been known worldwide for spices since time immemorial. In the 17th century, India started the development of crops, majorly maize and tobacco. Farmers of the Bengal began the cultivation of mulberries and developed sericulture (the production of silk and rearing silkworms for producing silk). Indian agriculture was advanced compared to Europe. The Mughal era induced and made more emphasis on agrarian reforms with the establishment of irrigation systems.

Industrial development began with spinning, weaving and manufacturing companies in Bombay (now Mumbai) through the well-known entrepreneur Jamsetji Tata. Other mills were also existing that produced yarn for making clothes.

Exporting cotton and silk to larger markets of America, Africa, Asia, and Europe was broad in the 1750s. British era did affect the Indian trade system. Indian textile industry was manipulated by them, and they made British industries pay taxes for importing Indian textile. They slowly let British textiles enter the Indian markets and increased the value of imports heavily. Many movements broke out, the famous Swadeshi and Boycott movements for adopting Indian products and textiles and refraining from buying British and other foreign goods for self-reliance and improvement of domestic trade.

Many other items of trade were discovered, such as coal mines. The East India Company established maps for identifying available natural resources throughout the territory of India with the help of a Geological Survey. The iron and Steel Industry rose after the mid of the 19th century. The establishment of metal roads for expanding trade networks took place hand-in-hand. Other industries, such as paper manufacturing, publications, were established. There were also chemical refineries established in India to produce petrol, paints, kerosene, and other chemicals of everyday usage.

- **Constitutional provision for Trade and Commerce**

Article 19 (1) (g):

Every citizen of India is provided with the right to practice a profession of their choice, carry out trade and businesses freely. This provision is given under Fundamental Rights, Article 19 (1) (g) of the Constitution. However, this right has some restrictions on public interest. If the nature of any profession, trade, or business is not lawful or if the law identifies such a job as against the public policy, then such job cannot be carried on further. It is also to be noted that any job, occupation, business, or trade must not obstruct the working of any government statutory body. For the proper understanding of the provision, the essential terminologies are explained:

Profession: refers to an occupation that includes a more extended period of training for acquiring the required knowledge to achieve excellence in the particular profession. Entry into any profession is restricted through examinations, such as a lawyer is required to clear the Bar Exam for acquiring the license to practice law.

Occupation: refers to any job title acquired through required qualifications, such as a manager who has completed MBA or an IT engineer who has completed Computer Science Engineering.

Trade: in simple terms, trade means buying and selling goods and services. In more broad terms, trade requires special skills for conducting the job of selling goods. Trade involves selling pf goods in exchange for money. Trade can take place between businesses, business to customers, and between customers as well.

Business: it is defined as any firm or enterprise, or organization that works for achieving some objective. Carrying out a business is a massive task as it involves various facets, such as market interests, public interests, restrictions and requirements of the government, profit, costs of productions, raw materials. An example of business can a publishing company; the main objective of running a publishing company will be to publish books, journals, magazines while earning a suitable and sufficient amount of profit.

Commerce: it includes the exchange of goods and services, and unlike trade, it is an extensive area. It involves macroeconomic sales and purchases made by large organizations. Commerce comes under business and is majorly focused on distribution rather than production.

Clause (6) of Article 19 describes that the State can impose reasonable restrictions for the public interest on the right provided under sub-clause (g) of clause (1) of Article 19. It is further stated that to practice any profession, trade, occupation, or business, professional or technical qualifications are prescribed, and the State can carry on any business or trade of choice by either excluding the citizens wholly or partially.

It is necessary to allow trade with proper control for healthy competition to avoid conflicts and chaos. Proper regulations are required to be implemented so that all traders, business houses and other professionals involved in trading can carry out their occupation freely. Traders involved in hawking are included in the provision, and they cannot be denied that they are working on the streets; they must be regulated with proper provisions of the Constitution, and their rights must also be protected [2].

It is significant to note that to sell liquor in India, one need to acquire a license. It is the State's responsibility, and for the very purpose of preventing dangerous products from being sold to the public at large, the police are provided with the power to take the necessary actions. The State has powers for ensuring that the sale and manufacture of intoxicating liquors are prohibited. However, this does not mean that sale of liquor is illegal; if proper licenses and other legal requirements are done accordingly; one is free to manufacture and sell liquor. It must also be noted that in India, the State has the right to manufacture and sell liquor.

- **Part XIII of the Constitution**

Article 301:

Article 301 of the Constitution defines freedom of trade, commerce, and intercourse. It states that trade, commerce, and intercourse is accessible throughout the territory of India. The Indian Constitution has adopted Section 92 of the Australian Constitution as Article 301, which describes that trade, commerce, and intercourse between the states must be free whether it is done through road or ocean or any other means [3].

This provision of the Constitution was initially intended to remove State custom barriers. Customs barrier means charging fees or implementing rules for limiting trade. However, later on, this intention was changed due to judicial reviews and decisions. Now, it is applicable for states and well the commonwealth [4].

The provision of Article 301 is applicable for inter-state as well as intra-state trade purposes. It is important to note that Article 301 states that it is free to carry on a trade or business of choice, but that does not mean that one is free from the laws. Any regulatory law cannot become a violative law. Laws are specially made to ensure that people abide by the regulations, and application of any law cannot be violative; of course, there are exceptions. For example, levying tax does not act as a barrier to trade or cannot be called Article 19 (1) (g) or Article 301 are both considered infringing.

Article 302:

Article 302 talks about the power of the Parliament for the imposition of restrictions on Article 301. Article 302 states that the Parliament can impose mandatory restrictions on the freedom of trade, commerce, or intercourse between one State and another within multiple states or within any part of the territory as it thinks fit [5].

This article delegated authority to the Parliament to impose restrictions for the public interest. By restrictions, it must be inferred that the freedom of trade in the territory of India is restricted. The Parliament is free to impose such restrictions in inter-state and intra-state business transactions, trade, or commerce.

This provision was widely explained by the Sarkaria Commission clearly. The explanation states that some situations might arise where it is necessary to impose restrictions on trade and commerce activities. In a country like India with a vast economy and cultural diversity, it becomes the responsibility of the Centre to regulate trade and commerce activities in certain situations. For example, the need to protect the natural resources of various states from getting exploited. Natural resources are used for trade and business, and other related activities, so it is the ultimate responsibility of the Centre to ensure their availability and prohibiting their exploitation. It is also further explained that it is significant that the Parliament controls intra-state trade in situations where production takes place only in one State, but the distribution of the products is done to different states [6].

Article 303:

Clause (1) of Article 303 states that neither the Parliament nor the Legislature of any start has the power to make any law in favour of one particular State or authorizing the making of any such law as it becomes discriminatory on other states. Clause (2) of Article 303 states that if a situation arises in any state, such as goods scarcity, and the Parliament finds it necessary to make such law as mentioned in clause (1), the Parliament can do so.

In case of law, the Supreme Court once again refused to explicit an opinion in the well-known query, or even at the confined question whether, for the provisions of Article 303, entries referring to Tax on Sale of Goods Act (Section 92A) are referring to trade and commerce. It was argued that because it hampered trade and commerce via means of providing choice to at least one State over another or utilizing discrimination among one State and another, In State of Madras v. Nataraja Mudaliar, it was alleged that Arts. 301 and 303(1) were violated because they impeded trade and commerce by favouring one State over another or discriminating between one State and another. The Court rejected the claim, finding that an Act adopted for the "purpose of imposing a tax to be collected and kept by the State "does not amount to a law favouring one State over another or discriminating between them simply because of various tax rates in different states. Several reasons were adduced in support of this view.

First, the flow of trade does not necessarily depend upon the sales tax rates, and various other factors also are relevant. Secondly, referring to the Australian cases, the Court derived the principle applicable in the present case, viz., "where differentiation is based on considerations not dependent upon natural or business factors which operate with more or less force in different localities that the Parliament is prohibited from discriminating." Thirdly, by leaving it to the State from which the movement of goods commences to levy Central sales tax on the sale, at rates prevailing in the State, no discrimination can be deemed to be practiced. "It is clear that the legislature has contemplated that elasticity of rates consistent with economic forces is intended to be maintained."

The approach of the Court in Nataraja appears to have been influenced by the fact that the Central sales tax is to be levied by the State of export; that it is in the interest of such a State to fix such rates of sales tax as may not discourage prospective buyers, and this would discourage the State from imposing an unduly high rate of sales tax. The question of a State of import is, however, covered explicitly by Art. 304 (a). Though the scheme of the Central Act was held valid in the Nataraja case, nevertheless, there appears to be little doubt that if the Central Act had itself levied differential rates of sales tax (and not left it to the States to fix the rate then it would have been invalid because of Art. 303. As the Act, itself did not do anything like this and merely left the matter to the States. It can be argued that the Centre was not indulging in any discrimination between State and State. Moreover, by equating intra-State and inter-State commerce as to the rates of taxation, even a state cannot be accused of discriminating against interstate trade. [7].

Article 304:

Clause (a) of Article 304 states the Legislature of any State can impose a tax on goods that are imported from other states where similar goods are produced. Clause (b) of Article 304 states that the Legislature of a State can impose reasonable restrictions on the provisions as mentioned under Article 301 with any other state or within the State for public interest if necessary.

It must be noted that the Legislature of any state is not allowed to introduce any bill or make any amendment without the prior consent of the President. Article 304 does not restrict the levying of tax on goods but restricts the levy of the tax on goods that would be seen as discriminatory between goods that were imported from other States and similar goods that were produced. The main objective is that the tax levied on local goods and on imported goods from other states must be the same.

In this case, Madhya Pradesh imposed a sales tax on the sale of tobacco sold in the State by a merchant by importing. Importing tobacco without help from anyone else was not liable to burden, and if the imported tobacco was not sold in the State, no tax was payable. Still, the Supreme Court held that the tax being referred to straightforwardly obstructed exchange and trade between Madhya Pradesh and different States. The duty was not saved by clause (a) of Article 304 because tobacco manufactured or produced inside Madhya Pradesh was not dependent upon any charge. Thus that tax was unconstitutional [8].

Article 305:

Article 305 includes the provision for saving the existing laws and providing the laws for State monopolies. It states that the provisions of Articles 301 and 303 will not affect any other existing laws. The only exception is when the President directs any changes. Also, Article 301 does not affect any other law made before the 4th Constitutional (Amendment) Act, 1955.

In a case [9],it was questioned by the Supreme Court that does State monopoly for few trade and commerce activities violate the provision of Article 301 and 19 (1) (g) or not. The question was left undecided. The judgment inferred that even after the first amendment to take out such state monopolies, no other provision was added to Article 305. Thus, even though the amendment was made, if any law that makes such state monopoly, it must be justified before the Court that such is done for in public interest, is not violative of freedom of trade and commerce, and falls under reasonable restrictions under clause (b) of Article 304 of the Constitution.

After the fourth Constitutional Amendment, existing laws and future laws that include state monopoly for any trade or commerce activities are not violative of Articles 301 and 303.

Article 307:

Article 307 explains the appointment of authority to carry out the provisions of Articles 301 to 304 smoothly. Article 307 states that the Parliament can appoint such authority it thinks fit for fulfilling and carrying out the provisions as mentioned and explained under Articles 301 to 304. Parliament can confer powers and duties it thinks fit on such authority as appointed.

· **Case Laws**

In the case *Atiabari Tea Co. v. State of Assam*[10],the petitioner was into the transportation of tea to Calcutta through Assam. During the transportation to Calcutta, the tea was liable to tax in Assam. It was questioned that whether this violates the provision given under Article 301 of the Constitution and whether it can be protected under clause (b) of Article 304. The Supreme Court held that levying the tax, in this case, is infringing the movement of goods. Thus, this will fall under Article 301, and the Act under which such tax was levied was held void.

In another case, *Sukumar Mukherjee v. State of West Bengal*[11],the appellant argued that there were unreasonable restrictions imposed on the right as given under Article 19 (1) (g) of the Constitution of India. The restriction was imposed by Section 9 of the West Bengal State Health Act, 1990, which prohibited teacher doctors working at West Bengal Medical Education Service (WBMES) from practising privately. However, the restriction was teacher doctors of WBMES and not on doctors of the West Bengal Health Service (WBHS). The Court held that such restriction was reasonable because when one has decided to work for the government, they are bound by the terms and conditions of service to the government.

Article 47 of the Constitution of India describes that the State must increase the nutrition level and standard of living of the people and focus on improving health as one of its primary duties. It is the responsibility of the State to prohibit the consumption of intoxicating beverages and substances that are harmful to one's health, unless for medical reasons[12]. The application of Article 47 along with Article 19 (1) (g) was made in a case[13]where liquor business was prohibited. The controversy was whether it is a fundamental right of a citizen to trade or carry on a business in liquor. The Supreme Court held that even though we have the freedom of trade and Commerce under Article 19 (1) (g), they are not absolute, and the State has the authority to impose reasonable restrictions. It is further held that citizens do not have the fundamental right to do a business that deals in goods that are injurious to the health and safety of the public.

It is another significant restriction of Article 19 (1) (g) that one professional is restricted entry into another profession. In a case, *Dr Haniraj L. Chuhani v. Bar Council of Maharashtra and Goa*, [14] the appellant, who was a doctor by profession, had applied for enrolling as an Advocate. The rules under the Bar Council prohibited him from such enrolment. This made the appellant challenging the validity of Article 19 (1) (g) of the Constitution of India. The appellant argued that he was entitled to practice as an advocate even though he was a doctor and practice both professions simultaneously. However, the Supreme Court held that one person could not practice two or more professions at one time. It was further held that the State Bar Council's rule prohibiting entry of a person who is already a professional to enrol for the bar is justified.

In the case, *B. R. Enterprises v. State of Uttar Pradesh*, [15]the petitioners claimed that the Lotteries (Regulation) Act, 1998 and the order passed by the State of Uttar Pradesh is violative of Articles 301, 302 and 303 of Part XIII of the Constitution of India. The order passed by the State of Uttar Pradesh stated that the sale of lottery tickets from other states is banned. The Supreme Court held that a lottery could not be considered a business or commerce but gambling. Thus, the order passed is not violative of Articles 301, 302, and 303. The significant difference between trade and gambling (lottery as in this case) is that trade involves skills, whereas gambling involves only chance (in simple words, luck). Therefore, the ban on lottery tickets from other states in Uttar Pradesh is not violative of Article 19 (1) (g) or part XIII of the Constitution.

The establishment of educational institutions is neither trade nor commerce nor business. It was held in a case [16] that trade or business generally has profit as the main objective, but education is a service and does not intend to earn profit.

In a country like India, with religious diversity, many animals are worshipped, and the cow is one. Cattle are also considered anessential contributor to agriculture which automatically helps in economic growth. In a case,[1] the butcher petitioners had filed a petition that Section 5 of the Bombay Animal Preservation Gujrat Amendment Act, 1994 that is applicable in Gujrat, is violative of Article 19 (1) (g) and Part XIII of the Constitution of India. They argued that the Act imposes a ban on the slaughter of cows, calves and other milch cattle thus, violating the right of the butchers to practice an occupation of their choice freely. The Supreme Court held that the Act imposes a ban only on a particular class of cattle only and not all types of cattle, the butchers are free to slaughter cattle that are not mentioned under the said Act, and it was concluded that the Act is not violative of freedom of trade and commerce.

In *Indian Cement v. State of Andhra Pradesh*[17],the petitioners argued that the notification issued by the State of Andhra Pradesh and Karnataka under Section 8 (5) of the Central Sales Tax Act, 1956 was violative of Part III of the Constitution of India, the reason being that the reduction of the tax rate on the sale of cement by local cement manufactures did not benefit the cement manufacturers from other states who had their sales officers in Andhra Pradesh. The Supreme Court held that Section 8 (5) of the Central Sales Tax Act, 1956 was violative of Part III of the Constitution of India and were liable to be repealed.

· Conclusion

Fundamental Rights are the most important for every citizen. Freedom of Trade is one of them. This right gives access to the citizens to practice any profession, occupation, a business of their choice. This is a fundamental right as it helps build a source of income for the citizens and the development of the economy for the nation. Article 19 (1) (g) under Part III of the Constitution and Articles 301 to 307 under Part XIII of the Constitution talks widely about the Freedom of Trade, Commerce, and Intercourse. It must be noted that this freedom is not absolute and holds reasonable restrictions that can be imposed. Such restrictions are not violative of the provisions mentioned and explained in this paper. Over the years many cases, regarding violation of such provisions have taken place, and in most cases, the Courts have given sound judgments. The freedom of trade and commerce is protected, and no one can violate such rights.

- **References**

1. Bowie, Studies in Federalism, p. 296-357 (1954).
2. Sodan Singh v. NDMC AIR 1988 SC (1988).
3. J.N. Pandey, Constitutional Law of India, p. 763 (Central Law Agency, Allahabad, 58th edn. 2020).
4. James v. Commonwealth of Australia (1936) AC 578.
5. Article 302 of the Indian Constitution, available at: https://indiankanoon.org/doc/412767/ (Visited on August 22nd, 2021). State of Madras v. Nataraja Mudaliar, AIR 1969 SC 147: (1968) 3 SCR 829; supra.
6. State of Madhya Pradesh v. Bhailal Bhai, AIR 1964 SC 1006: (1964) 6 SCR 261.
7. Saghir Ahmad v. State of Uttar Pradesh, AIR 1956 SC 728.
8. AIR 1961 SC 232.
9. (1993) 3 SCC 724.

౫

III

Revisiting The Appointment in Higher Judiciary and Judicial Independence

Authored By: Nidhi Nande

Third Year Student of Symbiosis Law School, Pune

· **Abstract**

The framers of our Constitution, while drafting the Constitution, were of the view that the Judiciary should be independent of the executive and should be competent in its own. In the light of such views,specific provisions were made in the Indian Constitution to provide for the appointment of judges, their tenure, their transfer and many more. However, there are recent debates about the appointment of judges and the process adopted in the country. The paper starts by understanding the parliamentary dilemma on the issue and revisits the models of appointment in higher Judiciary through the judges' case, and critically analyses the collegiumsSystem as well as the NJAC. The paper suggests other mechanisms taking into account a global perspective concerning the appointment models of other countries.

· **Keywords:***Constitution,Judiciary, amendment, law, independence*

- **Literature review**

The present review of literature studies the research work done by various researchers on judicial independence, collegiumsSystem, the unconstitutionality of NJAC and the appointment in higher Judiciary in India and globally, which is of paramount importance in the research endeavour. Attempts have been made in this paper to draw meaningful guidelines from the past research and gather various objectives, results and conclusions on appointment in higher Judiciary and its judicial Independence, which would help us enhance the current legal structure of our country and upgrade our laws to make it up to the international standards.

a. Singh M.P. 2000 studied **"Securing the Independence of Judiciary- The Indian Experience",** in which he highlighted the role judiciary played in enhancing its independence despite all the troubles and tribulations India faced since the commencement of the Constitution. The paper gave a walk through the three judges case and their implementations. It also studied the growing unease felt and expressed in the context of Judicial Independence and Judicial Accountability. In the end, it was concluded by the author that the democratic Constitution can survive in a better way due to the independence given to the Judiciary in India, and it is therefore expected to protect, preserve and promote the Independence of the Judiciary (Singh, 2000).

b. Purushothaman, Purush studied **"Higher Judicial Appointments in India- The Dilemma and the Hope: Trusting the Wisdom of Generations"** (Purush, 2013), in which it was stated in the context of the appointment of higher Judiciary, the conflict that arose between the judicialindependence and its accountability. It also highlighted the instances when either the executive or the Judiciary was given primacy in opinion and the resultant havoc created in the System. The paper concluded with the suggestion of creating sound constitutional pacts in the System which would ensure the stability of both judicial autonomy and self-governing accountability.

c. Tiwari Neeraj (2009) studied **"Appointment of Judges in Higher Judiciary: An interpretational Riddle",**in which the divergence from the original System in the appointment of higher Judiciary, which was supposed to consist of the consultative process, is discussed. The paper studied how from 1993(the second judges' case), the original System was wholly discarded, and most of the power in the judicial appointment was held in the hands of the Judiciary. The paper concludes by emphasizing the need to re-evaluate the current System of appointment and upgrade the laws regarding the matter.

d. Bhatia, Gautam (2016) studied**"The Primacy of Judges"**,in which the Primacy of Opinion of judges was revisited considering the appointment of Judges in Higher Judiciary. The paper vastly analyses the NJAC judgment finding loopholes in the relation of the primacy of opinion and unconstitutionality of NJAC. The paper finally concludes with the importance of judicial primacy of opinion.

e. Das Cyrus (2004) studied **"Judges and Judicial Accountability"** in which he described that the judges of Higher Judiciary are accountable in themselves as they are treated as the trustees of the people and thus are supposed to work as per the standards of their position in order to be responsible for their conduct.

- **Scope and object**

The appointment of judges, which was originally supposed to be a consultative process, has, by the effects of some external forces, destabilized the balance between the executive and Judiciary even since the process of appointment of judges has undergone various criticism. It has been subject to a variety of judicial interpretations. Although the provisions relating to the appointment of judges are very clear in the Constitution, the major concern arises from its implementation, which does not align with the ideals framed by the constitution-makers. In particular, the vagueness and devoid of transparency of the System has led to examining the legal structure on the matter. Another main object of the research is to clarify the gap between judicial autonomy and its responsibility and the hampering of judicial independence in the appointment process.

- **Hypothesis**

The work is guided by the following hypotheses:

- The appointment of judges does not provide enough room for discussion in the matters of strengths and weaknesses of the judges recommended due to the lack of transparency and the tussle between executive and Judiciary.

- The ineffectiveness of the Collegium system in the process of appointment.
- The question of independence and accountability of the Judiciary in India.

· Research methodology

The methodology adopted for the research is descriptive, doctrinal, and analytical. The research work is mainly based on secondary sources like books, articles, journals, and other research works. It is a mixture of theoretical work which is based on the information gathered from books, articles, and the Constitution of India and thereby analysis and criticism of the information gathered by the author. A comparative analysis is also made better to understand the position of the Indian Legal System vis-à-vis the Legal System of other countries, which also helped the author recommend various alternatives for the country. Wherever there has been any remark about any institution, it has been made only with the motive of upholding the dignity and Democracy of the country.

· Introduction

> *"All the rights secured to the citizens under the Constitution are worth nothing and a mere bubble, except guaranteed to them by an independent and virtuous Judiciary."*
>
> *--- Andrew Jackson*

Our country India to establish a free and democratic society, has adopted a liberal Constitution in the Euro-American traditions, which aim at prosperity and stability of the people. Such a society could be created by completely guaranteeing the Fundamental Rights of the people, which in turn could only be achieved by ensuring an independent judiciary to safeguard those rights. Thus the framers of the Constitution considered these aspects with maximum and identical idealism.

The draft of the Constitution for this very purpose included a provision that separated the Judiciary from the executive. In this backdrop, the judicial appointment assumes significance which has been debated for so long between the legislature, Judiciary and executive, and it cannot be ignored that much of these conflicts have emerged from the need of maintaining the Independence of the Judiciary.

1. Independence of Judiciary

Independence of Judiciary is a concept that the Judiciary should be an independent body and should be free from other branches of the Government. It should have freedom from fear and favour of the other two organs. The concept has its origin in the doctrine of separation of powers. Defining the Independence of Judiciary by emphasizing only the creation of Judiciary as an autonomous institution separate from other branches is not sufficient unless the core idea of judicial independence is exhibited in its definition, which is the independent power of the judges to decide a case before them according to the rule of law uninfluenced by any other factors.

Independence of the Judiciary is important for the sole reason of safeguarding the rights and privileges of the people and thereby providing equity and justice to all. The rule of law, which explains the supremacy of the Constitution, can only be achieved when there is an independent and impartial judiciary at the top level to ensure proper interpretation and implementation of the Rule of Law. Due to these reasons, it becomes of utmost importance to maintain or improve the Independence of the Judiciary and thus protect the Democracy of the Indian System.

2. Parliamentary dilemma

The people of a country losing faith in its legislature and executive are still acceptable, but it would be the evilest day of the people start losing faith in its Judiciary. Judiciary is an institution that acts as a guardian of human and fundamental rights guaranteed to the people under the Constitution. Therefore, the framers of the Constitution, in its very first phase, realized the importance of a strong and independent judiciary in a country that has adopted a democratic form of Government with a federal system working for the welfare of the citizens. The Judiciary was supposed to be an arm of the social revolution that would uphold the equality and freedom of the people of India who have suffered these losses in their past during British Rule. The Constituent Assembly, therefore, ensured to make Judiciary an independent body with full powers of judicial review. The idea for the Independence of the Judiciary in the Indian Constitution has been largely influenced by the report of the Sapru Committee, which strongly criticized the unfettered discretion of the executive for the appointments of the higher Judiciary. The rationale behind the provision of the Union Constitution

Committee was to include the apolitical office of the Chief Justices for appointments along with the final words of the President as this would ensure the highest quality of judges to be appointed. The Constituent Assembly accepted the provision of the Union Constitution Committee along with making the consultation to the Chief Justice of India mandatory.

The importance of adequate checks and balances was also emphasized upon by TT Krishnamachari, who cautioned the excessive power of the Judiciary, which would otherwise become an "*Imprerim in Imperio, operating as a sort of superior body to the general body politic*". Responding to this view, B.R. Ambedkar highlighted two crucial aspects. First, the incorporation of consultation with the Chief Justice of India was not in any way meant to undermine the fundamental nature of the power of appointment, which rests with the executive. Rather, it was to ensure a necessary check in order to ensure the independence of the Judiciary. Secondly, the main emphasis was on inter-institutional balance in appointments between the Judiciary and executive, who would mutually check and inform each other. The main idea, which was then understood for ensuring the Independence of the Judiciary, has lost sight in the modern debates, which solely revolve around the judicial conflict with the executive to demonstrate independence.

A. An insight into the models of appointment in the Higher Judiciary

To better analyze the controversies regarding the appointment of the higher Judiciary and Independence of Judiciary, it becomes necessary to understand how judges were appointed in the higher Judiciary. The Constitution has incorporated the appointment of judges to the Supreme Court and High Court's in Article 124 and Article 217, respectively.According to these provisions, the President of India appoints Supreme Court judges in consultation with the Chief Justice of India (C.J.I.) and other Supreme Court and High Court judges as the President of India deems necessary. Furthermore, the President appoints judges to the High Courts in consultation with the Chief Justice of the United States, the Governor of the concerned state, and the Chief Justice of that High Court, as required by the Constitution.

The actual conflict rested in the word 'consultation' and its implications. The three judges' case acts as a landmark that sought to clarify the situation by its interpretation, thereby redefining the appointment of judges, Independence of Judiciary and Separation of powers.

1. **Keshavanand Bharti v State of Kerala[1]**

Keshavanand Bharti,by its judgment, established the doctrine of basic structure, which purports to protect the basic principles and values of the Constitution unaltered by the executive or any act of the legislature. The verdict was not well-received by the Government led by Indira Gandhi as they considered it to curtail their powers. This is where the genesis of the judge's case began in 1973 when one of the judges who dissented the majority opinion in the Keshavanand Bharti's case, Justice Ajit Nath Ray, was promoted to the position of Chief Justice of India, superseding the other three senior judges who had ruled in favour of the judgment. This way executive blatantly attacked the Independence of the Judiciary, and it, in retrospect, has been rightly called the black day for Indian Democracy.

2. **S.P. Gupta v Union of India[2](The first judges' case)**

From the day the Constitution was adopted to the year 1973, the President accepted the appointment of a higher Judiciary as per the recommendations of the Chief Justice of India and other judges. When Justice A N Ray was appointed, it was for the first time felt that the Independence of the Judiciary was undermined. For the first time in the case of Union of India v SakalchandHimmatlal Seth[3], the word consultation was considered to mean effective consultation upholding the spirit of Constitution.

The matters of additional appointments and reckless transfers from one High Court to another came to a head with the issuance of Circular by the Union Minister of Law and Justice in 1981, which acted as a more extensive executive interference in the appointment and transfer of judges.. The Supreme Court eventually heard all of these cases together in a case known as the First Judges Case. By a majority of 4:3, it was held that the word 'Consultation' in the Articles 124(2) and 217(1) of the Constitution does not mean concurrence in the light of the appointment of the judges and hence the ultimate power rests with the President and under Article 74 which implies that President works only after the consultation of the Council of Ministers.

The major criticism of the judgment was the wrong interpretation of effective consultation as the final word rested with the executive, the point of judicial opinion was rendered useless. Effective consultation would rather be understood as acceptance or non-acceptance of the recommendation of the Judiciary but with valid proof without claiming the parliamentary privilege of non-disclosure. Also, it committed disservice to its cause of independence by holding that the opinion of the Chief Justice of India was not supreme but acted only as a piece of advice.

3. Supreme Court Bar Association v Union of India, 1993 (The second judges' case)[4]

The mass scale corruption and favouritism in the appointment of Judiciary led to the second judges' case where the 11 judges' bench was formed to overrule the decision of 7 judges bench in the first judges' case. In this case, it was held that in the event of non-consensus between the Chief Justice and the President, the opinion of the Chief justice would be given primacy and would be determinative. Although the power of the executive was not altogether taken away on papers, practically in one way, they not only acquired in themselves the Independence of the Judiciary but also kicked out the executive role in the process of appointment. The word 'consultation' was meant after this case to take concurrence of the suggestion of judges by the President.

The major outcome of the case, which was expected to secure the balance of power between the Judiciary and executive,resulted in the judicial supremacy of powers in the appointment of higher judiciary and collegiums system to guard the charge of non-transparency and arbitrariness.

4. In re Special Reference 1 of 1998 (Third judges' case)[5]

When Chief justice M.M. Punchhi appointed other judges without consultation of any other judges, the Government of India asked President to approach Supreme Court to clarify this point. As a result, it was made clear that consultation in Article 217(1) and Article 222(1) means to consult with a plurality of judges. This case is also important because it gave the composition of the Collegium, which is followed even today, which consists of the Chief Justice of India along with four senior judges of the Supreme Court.

The result of this judgment was an inevitable pushback to the supreme power of the Judiciary in the appointment of judges. Also, there is an unwritten Veto power of the Chief Justice of India in matters of rejection.

5. **National Judicial Appointment Commission[6]**

The NJAC Bill was passed in 2014 by both the houses of parliament in the 99th Constitutional Amendment Bill, thereby declaring the collegiums System inoperative. The NJAC proposed to make the appointment of judges more transparent by appointing them through the members of the Judiciary, legislature and civil society, which consists of three members from the Judiciary, a law minister and two jurists. Through the NJAC amendment[7], Articles 124 A, B and C were added to the Constitution of India to make the amendment valid. A recent landmark judgment declared the NJAC unconstitutional[8]. The main holdings of the court concerning the unconstitutionality were about its violating of the basic structure of the Constitution by not maintaining judicial primacy, thereby affecting the Independence of Judiciary, which is a part of the basic structure.

The dissenting opinion in the NJAC judgment left some doors open for discussion. The judgment never explained why the primacy of the opinion of the Judiciary a necessary component of the Independence of Judiciary is. Also, the judge assumes that the judicial appointment affects the Independence of the Judiciary, which is based on the narrow definition of judicial independence. The definition does not consider the external bias and pressure which could affect the impartial judgment on the part of judges and, in turn, ruin the whole idea of Independence of the Judiciary. There are other democratic countries like United Kingdom, Canada,and South Africa where political figures control judicial independence without any detriment to judicial independence. The judgment failed to acknowledge that independence could be better assured where there is a consultative process of selection.

B. **Major concerns in the present model of judicial appointment**

Judge Jerome Frank stated that-

> *"In a democracy, it is never unwise to acquaint the public with the truth about the workings of any branch of Government. It is wholly undemocratic to treat thepublic as children who are unable to accept the inescapable shortcomings of manmadeinstitutions"(Frank,1973)*

When the NJAC was declared unconstitutional, the major point of concern was whether the collegium system is the best alternative or are their loopholes to it. On analyzing, it was found that the collegium system has in one way lost its legitimacy and is not a source to deliver impartial appointments. The Collegium system, although it provides the primacy of the Judiciary, it undermines the basic idea of appointment being a consultative process. Practically there exists no role of the President, and he merely acts as a postman appoints the judge selected by the Collegium. On understanding the approach of the Supreme Court, it can be implied that the Supreme Court seems to interpret too much in the provision that they end up making a new version of the provision, which was not the legislative intent at the time of framing of the provision. One of the biggest examplesof it has been the intricate guidelines given by the Supreme Court in the Third Judges' Case, which cannot be interpreted from the bare reading of the provisions of the Constitution of India.

Another major point is that the Government cannot reject the judge recommended by the Collegium for the second time, but the loophole is that there is no prescribed time limit by which the Government can accept or reject. This acts as a barrier to the Independence of the Judiciary wherein there is the scope of intentionally holding back the recommendation for a long period without any deliberation. The present process of appointment has also attracted critique for carrying the aspects of favouritism or nepotism, and it has been largely feared that it may result in the situations of the judicial aristocracy (Bhushan, 2009)

C. **Comparative study of judicial independence and appointment of judges: a global perspective**

India borrowed the Independence of the Judiciary from the United States. The independence and the power of judicial review in Germany go even beyond the powers of the Supreme Court of United States. However, when we look at the System of appointment in higher Judiciary in these countries, there is no primacy of the opinion of Judiciary even then has causedany detriment to the Independence of Judiciary. In the United Kingdom, the judges are appointed by the recommendation of the President and Deputy President on approval of the Lord Chancellor[9]. In the United States, the federal judge is appointed by the President in consultation with the Senate[10]. In Canada, the Governor-General is empowered by the

Constitution on consultation of the Privy Council to appoint Justices. In South, Africa an appointment is made by the President on the recommendation of the Judicial Service Commission after consultation with the Chief Justice[11]. In Germany, appointments are made by-election; half of them are elected by the executive and half by the legislature. The System of appointment in all these countries clearly shows judicial independence is more likely to emerge when there is a consultative form of selection, and there is no need for collegiums to ensure Independence of the Judiciary. There must be a balance of Judiciary, executive and legislature to ensure fair selection.

D. Conclusion

There are serious concerns about the Indian institutions that have eroded the dignity, efficiency, integrity and most importantly, the faith of people from its System, which implies that the sole hope for a common person rests in its judicial System. In such a situation to ensure Justice- Social, Economic and Political" it becomes of utmost importance to maintain the Independence of Judiciary. The present article unfolded the historic pathway that the appointment of judges has covered, along with the importance of the Independence of the Judiciary. The paper, on another note, critically analyzed the instances that took place from 1973 to the unconstitutionality of NJAC and the present-daySystem of appointment of judges. Despite the measure taken to ensure the Independence of the Judiciary, there are shortcomings to the present System. Although the present collegium system is outwardly free from executive interference, still there are issues of lack of transparency and accountability.

E. Recommendations

The judicial appointment in India has been suffering major criticisms in recent days. There is a need to revisit the appointment in higher Judiciary through Collegium and upgrade India's legal System. Following are certain recommendations which could add to the objective-

- **Transparency in Appointments**- the major changes that are required in the Indian System revolves around the transparency issue. An example of a country where fair and open competition is ensured is the System in the U.K, where vacancies are advertised. Then the selection process takes place, including the shortlisting, references, recommendations, consultation, panel discussion, report submission and lastly, the quality assurance. India can adopt such a process as it would not only make the appointment transparent but also increase the accountability of the Judiciary and reduce malpractices.

- **Recommendatory Guidelines**- there have been many committees formed and various recommendations made regarding the appointment of judges, but the courts do not adopt them. One of the major recommendations which should be adopted is the Report on Restatement of Values of Judicial Life, 1997, which would serve as guidelines for the judge to build in themselves an independent, strong, and respected Judiciary.

- **Performance Evaluation**- In India, the Supreme Court is the watchdog of the Democracy, so it should be made necessary to evaluate the performance of the judges to ensure their efficiencies and whether they are upholding the Rule of Law or not. Such an evaluation was suggested in a report by the Planning Commission Panel in the 12th Five Year Plan to ensure the formal check and sustain the sagging public confidence.

- **Accountability of the judges**- A system that would ensure the accountability of the judges about their actions and their performances would enhance the societal confidence in the judicial system of our country, which is an essential part of Democracy.

- **References:**

1. (1973) 4 SCC 225
2. AIR 1982 SC 149
3. AIR 1977 SC 2328
4. (1993) 4 SCC 409
5. AIR 1999 SC 1
6. Constitution (Ninety Ninth Amendment) Act, 2014, Gazette of India
7. The Constitution (Ninety-ninth) Amendment) Bill, 2014, Government of India (2014)
8. Supreme Court Advocates on Record v Union of India, (2016) 5 SCC 1

IV

The Emotional Brain and the Guilty Mind

Authored By: Ms Monika Sharma

Student, Mehr Chand Mahajan Dav College for Women, Chandigarh

- **Abstract**

"Crime is not a thing to be appreciated; it is an act strongly criticizedby society".

It is believed that no one is born a criminal, a condition that compels them to be. Crime is a stage created by law. Human criminal behavior results from a variety of social, biological, psychological, and economic factors. The criminal mind is naturally aggressive, easily distracted and acts on these traits. A criminal is a person who is guilty of a crime. Criminals have no sympathy for the lousy price system. Their minds see themselves as invincible, which attracts lies, deception as a way of life. They want quick results without effort. Family circumstances, peer pressure also play a role in their criminal behaviour. Socially, a crime includes deviant behaviour which violates social norms that define expected behaviour. This paper seeks to understand how social, political, psychological, and economic changes can change the criminal thinking process.

- **Keywords**:*Deviant behaviour, mental health, Family environment, Criminal mind*

· Introduction

Crime can involve violence, sex, drugs, discrimination, road rage, undeclared work, exploitation, burglary; it also includes illegal selling of guns and other weapons. Whereas criminology investigates these different types of crime and the deviantbehaviour to suggest ways in which crime can be prevented, they try to explain criminal behaviour and also identify them and support the victims. The dictionary meaning of crime"is an act committed in violation of a law prohibiting it or omitted in violation of a law ordering it" Etymologically, it has been derived from the Latin word *CRIMEN* which means accusation and *LOGIA* means to study. Criminology is the entire body of knowledge regarding crime as a *social phenomenon;* it includes within its scope the process of making laws,i.e. sociology of law of breaking laws.

· Research Methodology

This paper will examine the motivation for a person to commit a crime and examine the interpretations of the views of those people. It is an attempt to identify the relationship between social factors and personality traits and, in search of ways to improve.

· Deviant Behaviour

Behaviour is driven by thoughts and feelings, which give insight into the mind of every individual, producing qualities like attitudes and values. Human behaviour is formed by psychological factors, as personality types vary from person to person, reflecting different actions and behaviours. There are four sorts of behaviour: optimistic, pessimistic, trusting, and envious.Crime is an act of deviation that violates not only the norm but the law. The deviationis often as slight as picking someone's nose publicly or as big as killing. Consistent with sociologist Sumner, deviation may violate established social, cultural, or social norms, whether social norms, customs, or collaborative law (Sumner, 1906).In social terms, deviation refers to an act or behaviour that violates social norms, including a law enacted (e.g., crime). Although the practice has been violated, ethics can still be described as positive or acceptable. Procedural violations are often classified as two approaches, standard deviations and informal deviations. Organized deviations are often defined as a crime, which violates the principles of society. Informal deviations are minor violations that violate the unwritten rules of public health. The foremost necessary behaviour is moral. Under the informal deviation, much of it contradicts social norms.

(Macionis, John; Gerber, Linda (2010). Merton (1950) described five deviations from acceptingor rejecting social goals, namely:

A.**Innovators are** the answer to the difficulties created by our culture of emphasizing wealth and the lack of opportunities to get rich, making people "innovators" by engaging in the theft and trafficking of drugs. The designers accepted shared goals but rejected socially acceptable ways of achieving them. (e.g. financial success is achieved through crime). Merton argues that innovators, especially those who are associated with the same worldviews as conformists, are not denied the opportunities they need to be able to achieve public goals legally.

B. **Conformists**-embrace community goals and acceptable ways to achieve them (e.g. financial success is achieved through hard work). Merton says conformists are primarily middle-class people who have been able to find opportunities in society as better education for financial success through hard work.

C. **Cultural historians refer** to the failure to achieve artistic goals and thus to adopt laws until the people in question lose their main goals in order to feel respected. Ritualists reject the motives of society but accept the ways of society. Ritualists are primarily found in dead, repetitive occupations, where they cannot achieve social goals but continue to follow social norms of gain and social norms.

D.**Retreatists**- are a rejection of both cultural goals and methods to allow the person in question to "leave the floor". Retreatants reject public goals and legitimate means of achieving them. Merton sees them as actual heretics, as they do deviant acts to achieve things that are not always in harmony with society's values.

E. **Rebels**- are almost like going back because the people in question also reject both cultural goals and methods but go one step further into "counterculture" in support of other existing public orders (the law violates). Rebels reject social goals and legitimate means of achieving them and instead create new policies and strategies to replace those of the community, not only creating new goals of achievement but also new ways of achieving the goals that other rebels will find acceptable.

Psychopathy and sociopaths- Psychopath and sociopath both refer to personality disorders that include anti-social behaviour, decreased sensitivity, and a lack of prevention. The term psychopath is often used to emphasize that the source of the disease is internal, depending on psychological, biological, or genetic factors. In contrast, sociopaths are used to highlighting the social features that characterize the disease: social or family resources for its development and social or legal inclusion (Hare, 1999). In this sense, sociopaths can be a social disorder by prominence. It includes the inability to be socius, but many social accounts describe them as lovable, attractive, and outgoing (Hare 1999).

- ## Characteristics of Criminal Human Mind

1. **Hypocrisy** - this practice is common and customary among criminals. Failure to regulate one's behaviour by beating may be a dominant thing about the criminal. Often they do not control their temper, which frequently results in tragic consequences like murder, violence against children and ladies, robbery and theft.

2. **Disruption** - the criminal's mind is distracted, often losing specialize in their legitimate purpose. The lack of remaining focused and targeted with their socially acceptable goals often leads the criminal to return to their old patterns. For instance, if a criminal is released from prison, he will return to an equivalent practice and believe he has been corrected.

3. **Invincibility**- the mind of the criminal resides within the concept "I will never be caught" and that they often believe that because a particular strategy has worked for them within the past, it will add the longer term and therefore, the result is going to be fruitful within the present. However, this often does not work, and that they often spend time in prison.

4. **Family unemployment** - the main feature of the perpetrator is that the emotional and financial absence of the family. Relationsthat do not support criminals and do not offer help often lead criminals to depression, anxiety that results in a white plague.

5. **Social value system** (compassion) - the criminal mind is insensitive to anyone, wholly alienated from social, social, and even relations. They live miserable life, grievances, and even this social life results in suicide. Presumably suicide.

6. **Redemption** - people living a criminal life tend to correct their behaviour by changing suspicion and questioning the motives of others.

For instance, if a lady did not want her purse stolen, she should are smart enough and would have locked the car. As a part of the rehabilitation of the criminal mind, he has never examined his behaviour.

7. Independent, criminal mindset is usually with the motto "me-me and me". They think they need a desire to try to do anything because life is usually about them.

- **Factors Contributing To Criminal Human Mind Are**

- Sociological factor
- Economic factor
- Psychological factor
- Biological factor

a. **SOCIOLOGICAL THEORY**

The view of the premier

Definition - "Crime is an act that is dangerous to society or believed to be dangerous to society by a group of people who have the power to enforce their beliefs and to place such an act under penalty of perjury." (John Gillin)

Factors-
- Anger and self-control
- Poor parenting in the family, marital problems, single-parent families, parental crime
- School experience — bad or wrong at school, poor academic performance
- Friends of the same age
- Unemployment, low pay, unpaid work
- Energy inequality
- The child's form of entertainment
- Social risk level (disorder, social control, opportunities)

Sociology encompasses a wide range of perspectives but often views crime as a social norm and emphasizes the cultural and social values of criminal behaviour—sociologists emphasize social groups and social structures that influence mortality. Many social theories of crimethink that it is a place that affects the criminal behaviour of a person and not the physical structure, as we know that humans were not born to be criminals. Social perceptions often focus on the relationship between crime and social inequality, peer pressure, inability to achieve social success. There are many ideas under the social aspect.

A. **Chicago School Thought-** A group of sociologists formed it in the 1920s who lived in the Chicago area. They wanted to find out if there was a relationship between the crime rate in the area and the characteristics of the area. The Chicago school has gathered substantial evidence from urban slums, citing the link between poverty and high crime rates. Poverty conditions include inadequate housing and a lack of economic opportunities, failure of school systems. Neighbours with high crime rates also have social unrest and lack trust.

B. **The View of Society Failure-**The perception of social unrest is based on Henry McKay and Clifford R. Shaw of the Chicago school. The concept of social order states that poverty-stricken and economically disadvantaged areas often meet high levels of human capital. These areas tend to have high human heterogeneity. With high incomes, the informal social structure often fails to grow, making it difficult to maintain social order in society. Society is in shambles that leads to social unrest and an increase in crime—deterioration of public controls. High school dropout rates, unemployment, deteriorating infrastructure, single-parent families, substance abuse, according to their research, poverty was most common in inner-city areas.

- **Objectives that were seen and required improvement;**

    1. Development of remote low-income areas.
    2. Lack of joint social opportunities
    3. Racial and ethnic discrimination

- **Social disorder**

    1. Deterioration of public institutions and organizations such as schools and families
    2. Lack of social control

- **Deterioration of social control**

    1. The development of gangs and gangs
    2. Peer groups enter into family and social spaces

- **Crime zones**

  1. A neighbour becomes a criminal
  2. Strengthening crime packs
  3. Lack of external support and investment

- **Carriers of crime**

1. Most youths grow old because of crime, get married, and raise a family, but some resort to crime only.

C. **Labeling Theory**

The idea for the label refers to someone who has been labelled in a certain way and read in great detail by Howard Becker. It comes from the beginning but is often used in crime studies. If a person is given a criminal label, he or she can be rejected or accepted and continue committing a crime. Even those who initially reject the label may end up accepting it as the label becomes even more profound when the labels are about deviations and are said to lead to increased deviations. Klein (1986) conducted an experiment that showed that the label's beliefs affected some perpetrators but not others. The central concept of collaborative labelling is a sign that people become criminals through contact with the criminal justice system (Becker 1963). Adding to this understanding of social research on the social characteristics of those incarcerated or under investigation by the criminal justice system - such as gender, age, race, and class — it appears that social variability and power structures are vital to understanding that it chooses a criminal approach. People who believe they are part of a community are less likely to commit crimes. Hirschi (1969) identified four types of social bonds that connect people to society:

1. Attachment measures our communication with others. The closer we get to people, the more we become concerned about their views of us. People adhere to social norms to gain approval (and prevent disapproval) from family, friends, and romantic partners.

2. Commitment means the investment we make per normal conduct. A well-respected businesswoman who volunteered for her synagogue and a member of an organization that blocks neighbours has much to lose by committing a crime rather than an unemployed woman or community obligations. There is a calculation of costs/benefits in a criminal decision

where arrest costs are much higher for some than for others.

3. Similarly, levels of involvement, or participation in legal activities in the community, reduce the chances of conversion. Children who are members of Little League baseball teams have fewer family problems.

D. **Strain Theory** -Strain theory is sociological and criminology theory developed in 1938 by Robert K Merton. This theory attempts to explain the causes of crime. The theory is that society puts pressure on individuals to achieve socially acceptable goals, even though they have no means. This leads to difficulties that can lead to the person committing a crime. He has taken up two areas, namely, cultural objectives and social structure. Cultural goals are those that are socially accepted by the economy, position and political power. It is a social structure and provides a means of reaching out to the community for artistic goals. Like education, investment and hard work. Merton's theory of oppression emphasizes financial success as the ultimate goal of culture. Opportunities are not shared equally in society; this is the cause when some people turn to illegal means to achieve these goals. So how do people adapt to these conditions?

- Conformist - embraces the goals and methods of success; for example, most students end up choosing science even though they have no interest in any subject. They may choose to do so because of peer pressure or the pressure from their parents to do so.

- The founder - accepts the terms but refuses to get there, for example dealing with drugs to achieve financial success.

- Cultural scholars - reject principles but accept methods, political practices that occur when people participate in a political process by voting even though they believe the system is broken and cannot achieve its goals.

- Retreatants - reject both objectives and methods,

- Apostates - want to replace the existing goals and strategies with their system

· **Types of genre**

- Built-in - refers to social norms that identify and influence one's perception of one's needs. If, in particular, social structures are inherently adequate or there is insufficient regulation, this can change a person's perception of ways and opportunities.

- Individual - this refers to the conflicts and pains experienced by a person as he seeks ways to satisfy his own needs. If public goals are essential to a person, achieving them may be more critical than accepted methods.

Conflict Theory-The idea of conflict is attributed to Karl Marx, a 19th-century political philosopher. The concept of social conflict is a broad-based social analysis. The conflict theory draws its attention to the division of power as a conflict of classes and generally compares historically prominent ideas. The theory is based on the assumption that conflicts between classes of society lead to crime. Conflict is created by capitalism and competition for scarce resources. Karl Marx argued that the law was defined by the people who control wealth and discriminates against the poor and that the criminal justice system is a way of controlling the poor. The conflict theory is based on the fundamental notion that the fundamental causes of crime are social and economic forces operating in society. Marx used the term "lumpenproletariat" to describe a layer that is unlikely to reach the stage. He mentioned the rich, who control the production and business processes, the capitalists. He noted the workers who relied on the capitalists to hire and survive the working class. Marx believed that the capitalists strengthened their power and influence by using the government, laws, and other authorities to maintain and expand their public office. Although Marx did not talk much about apostasy, his views formed the basis for the controversy over heresy and wealth.

F. **The View of Social Learning** - Social learning is a branch of ethical ideology closely linked to the crime. Social studies theorists, especially Albert Bandura, say that people are not born with the ability to be violent but that they are learning to be aggressive through their life experiences - Anger, in this case, one learns that is not known and requires experience

Condition of view of social learning behaviour

1. All behaviour is learned; deviant behaviour is studied in the same way as other behaviours.

2. Direct parental control; Albert reports that family health research shows that children who use aggressive tactics have parents who use similar tactics when interacting with others.

3. Another influence on social media reports is environmental violence. People living in areas where violence is a daily barrier are more likely to be violent than those living in low-crime areas.

4. Another source of moral change for many media. Movies and television programs often graphically portray violence. Moreover, in anticipation of such exhibitions, violence is often portrayed as acceptable behaviour, especially for heroes who have never experienced legal

consequences for their actions.

The socialist theorist said the following four factors help to produce violence and aggression;

- An event that enhances arousal - such as provoking someone or provoking another by slapping or verbally abusing others.

- Aggressive skills - learn aggressive responses obtained by looking at others, in person or through the media.

- Expected consequences - the belief that violence will be rewarded in some way. Rewards can come in the form of reducing tension or anger, earning a particular financial reward, building self-confidence, or gaining the praise of others.

- Consistency of behaviour - the belief, derived from the view of others, that violence is justified and justified, given the circumstances of the situation.

Psychological Theory Psychological theories suggest several theories about the causes of crime. Most important are the ideas that examine the relationship between crime and individual personality, social factors, understanding and developmental factors. Psychological literature shows that the key variables that are expressed in the formation of individual traits, as well as any criminal tendencies, are the role played by parents in such matters as child-rearing, attachment, neglect, abuse, and parental independence or criminal behaviour.

Psychological Factors of Crime

- Mental health and criminal behaviour - abnormal behaviour, schizophrenia (a severe mental illness in which a person confuses the real world with the world of thought and often behaves strangely and unexpectedly.)

- Mental illness (disturbing environment, mood swings, premature awakening)

- Anger and violence

- Criminal personality and personality disorder - deviant environment (that behaviour that falls away from social norms)

- Mental disorders (anxiety, self-harm, urgency

- Psychopaths, psychopathic personality

- Sociopaths (human disagreements) these people often do not understand other people's feelings.

Why do people commit crimes? At the same time, we also think about why crime exists in our society! The justice system deals with these questions, and the criminal expert is trying to answer them. It is imperative to note that there are many different interpretations of why people commit crimes (Conklin, 2007); one of the essential explanations is based on psychological theories, which focus on the interplay between intelligence, humanity, learning and criminal behaviour. There are three theories under the psychological aspect: psychodynamic theory, behavioural theory and cognitive theory.

G. **Psychodynamic Theory**- Proponents of the psychodynamic theory suggest that human personality is governed by conscious psychological processes rooted in childhood. This idea was developed by Sigmund Freud (1856-1939), founder of psychoanalysis. According to him, the human personality consists of a three-dimensional structure

1. Identity document

2. Ego

3. Superintendent

The id is the first part of the human brain that exists at birth. Freud (1933) believed that the id represents the illicit drugs of diet, sex, and other necessities of life. Most importantly, the idea is that id is concerned with instant gratification or self-satisfaction while ignoring caring for others. This is also known as the principle of happiness. The second element of human personality is the ego, which is thought to grow at the beginning of human life. It is also known as the law of truth. Freud (1933) suggested that the ego compensates for the demand for the id by directing a person's actions or ways of keeping him within social boundaries. The third personality trait is the superego; it grows as one incorporates moral and social values; parents; and other important people, such as friends and other clergy members. The focus of the superego is moral. Superego works to determine the behaviour and actions of individuals. (Freud, 1933). Criminals have weak egos and depraved personalities.

H. **Behaviour Theory**-Ethical perception ends with people's actions done through learning, rather than focusing on the ignorant personality or mental development patterns produced in childhood. Behavioural theorists are concerned with the actual behaviour people engage with during their daily lives. A fundamental principle of moral teaching is that people change their behaviour according to how they respond to others. Behaviour is supported by rewards and extinguished adverse reactions or punishment. Life always experiences shape behaviour.

· Evaluation vision and Moral development

Mental-minded psychologists focus on psychological processes and that people perceive and psychologically represent the world around them and solve problems. The pioneers of this school were Wilhelm Wundt (1832-1920), Edward Titchener (1876-1927), and William James (1842-1920). Lawrence Kohlberg first applied the concept of moral development to crime. He found that people go through stages of moral development, where their decisions and decisions are made in matters of right and wrong for different reasons. Kohlberg (1958) stages of development are;

Step 1 - right to submit to the power and avoid punishment

Section 2- The right to take responsibility for oneself, meet one's needs, and leave the responsibility to others.

Step 3 - It is good to be good in the sense of having good motives, caring for others, and putting oneself in someone else's shoes.

Article 4 - the right to maintain the rules and regulations of the community and to work for the welfare of the community.

Article 5 - the right is based on the individual's rights in the community with agreed rules - a social contract.

Article 6- The right is a duty derived from the principles applicable to all humanitarian principles - justice, equality and respect for human life.

His research work shows that criminals tend to be in category one and category 2. At the same time, non-criminals have reached a higher stage of moral development. People in the lower classes are afraid of punishment, and people in the middle class are afraid of the reaction of family and friends. High-ranking people believe that they should serve others. which means universal rights.

Cognitive perception deals with various aspects of human perception

1. It focuses on psychological processes, how people view the world around them and problem-solving. How people organize their thoughts through laws results in criminal and non-criminal behaviour.

2. It looks at the stages of moral growth, assuming that criminals do not continue to go to great heights as they cannotempathize and are motivated to love themselves.

3. It helps describe socially or socially inconsistent behaviour.

4. Mental illness - other symptoms associated with behavioural violence, such as confusion or delusional emotions.

J. Economic Theory and Factors- Economic crime or fraud is a common term used to denote wrongdoing or criminal activity or an organization, which aims to bring financial gain or illegal profits. Corruption and bribery constitute the illegal use of legal office for personal gain. The embezzlement measures are aimed at legitimizing the detection of crime by separating their true origins.

(Global Economic Research, 2005). The economic vision of crime is based on the assumption that people respond appropriately to the costs and benefits of crime.

- **Economic Factors of Crime**

A. Unemployment - unemployment causes a person to continue in crime as he or she does not have the source of the money he or she usually travels in the wrong way.

B.Food, shelter and clothing - these are the necessities of life if this is not met by a person who will become accustomed to criminal activity.

C. Low or poor income - when people think that their income or income is not enough to meet their needs.

D. Education - education plays a significant role; an illiterate person cannot understand right and wrong. Uneducated people often have an increase in criminal activity.

E. Sometimes, a person is helpless and at the same time is very susceptible to wrongdoing and often commits crimes.

F. To maintain a luxurious lifestyle, rich people also often commit crimes as they seek to get richer.

K. The Rational Choice Theory-The concept of rational choice was first introduced by economists and later adopted by critique in the late 1970s. The idea of rational choice is the idea that people behave as they do because they believe that doing the things they have chosen is more beneficial than the cost. It means that people make wise choices based on their goals, and those decisions dictate how they behave. A rational view means that criminals are rational in making their decisions, and even though there are consequences to the fact that the benefits of committing crimes outweigh the punishment.

An excellent example of this would be the white-collar crime; let us say the owner of an investment bank decides to withdraw money from his client's accounts and hide the loss, and he takes the money to fund his luxurious life. A white-collar criminal prepares and evaluates the options we have chosen, deciding that the personal benefits of stealing money outweigh any possible investment. Another good example would be the burglary of two people who broke the law and decided to work together to arrange a night out during the family vacation. Burglars have decided to plan and carry out burglary by measuring methods and benefits and deciding to break the law despite being punished if caught.

The basic principles of logical choice

1. Humans are intelligent
2. They can think logically
3. Interested people
4. People make their own choices
5. Choosing the people whom do it affects their resources
6. Man cannot fully control the consequences of his decisions

Radical View Point And Radical Theory- Intense ideas (from the 1960s to the 1970s) include the Marxist (Karl Marx 1818-1883) analysis of a capitalist society that allows things to exist as billions and billions while most people live in poverty or by. Such fundamental economic differences reflect contradictions in how work is organized into destructive, cruel, and oppressive conditions. Crime is seen as a sign of class struggle, a form of ancient rebellion and criminals who behave like rebels without finding a clue.

Various kinds of economic frauds

- **Insurance fraud** - insurance fraud occurs when a person or organization makes false insurance claims for compensation or benefits.

- **Trafficking** - in the latest 2017, Mumbai police have seized rupees worth 50crore.

- **Invoice fraud** - this term refers to the payment of goods at a price that is lower or higher than the price at which they were sold or bought.

- **Cybercrime** - theft of communication services, data theft, fraud and fraud, fraud, fraud, sales and investment fraud, burglary, copyright crime.

- **Fraud to consumers** - manufacturers or sellers of goods and services and deceive their customers in many ways. They may provide them with defective products or fail to deliver goods and services entirely.

- **Bribery and Corruption** - Entrepreneurs donate extra money to public servants to get to work faster or do illegal work. Corruption can undermine investment in other countries.

M. **Biological theory of crime and factors** Biological perceptions of the causes of crime focus on the idea that the physical body, by hereditary genes, mutations, brain structures, or the role of hormones, influences a person's involvement in criminal behaviour. . A growing understanding of these processes suggests that certain biological factors, such as specific genes, a lack of blood vessels, low serotonin activity, malnutrition and environmental pollution can affect a person's tendency to criminal or anti-social behaviour. The challenge of the ecological concept of crime is to represent the complex interplay between inherited and natural features adequately. The answers given by biological theory include measures such as;

- **Maternal health** efforts to reduce smoking and drinking among pregnant women, thereby reducing vascular damage to the developing baby. And

- **Public health** efforts and policy responses to reduce alcohol and alcohol abuse by youth,heavy alcohol consumption during adolescence is linked to severe neurological damage and chronic dementia.

- **Biological factors**

- Low intelligence
- Improper diet
- Impulsiveness
- Inefficiency
- Neurobiology, structural and brain damage, peril cortex (head injury, congenital disabilities)
- Neurotransmitters, malfunction of neurotransmitters, low levels of serotonin and dopamine
- Hormone influences, low testosterone levels and premenstrual syndrome.
- Genetics, genetic discovery and character transfer.

N. **Biological Theories**

1.**Cesare Lombroso** (1835-1909)

Cesare Lombroso was an Italian criminal scientist and the founder of an Italian criminal school. He dismissed the old school definition, believing that crime was a human trait and that crime was inherited. In this belief, he established the VISION OF LOSS. Where the human body's constitution indicates whether a person is born a criminal or not, these born criminals fall back on the previous stage of evolution by body composition, mental strength and first-person nature. In making this view, he saw the physical features of the Italian prisoners and compared them to those of Italian soldiers. Features of crime Lombroso concluded that criminals are physically different. Physical features not used to identify prisoners are included; 1. Asymmetry or face or head, 2. Large monkey-like ears, 3. Large lips, 4. Curly nose, 5. Long arms, 6. Large jaw, 7. Prominent chin, 8. Excessive claws, 9. Excess excessive wrinkles on the skin. Lombroso has announced that men with five or more traits can be classified as born criminals. Women, on the other hand, needed only those who needed at least three of these factors in order to be born criminals. Lombroso also believed that tattoos were branded as criminals because they stood as evidence of immortality and pain.

2. Chromosome Theory of Crime

The idea of an extra Y chromosome is the belief that criminals have an extra chromosome, giving them an XYY chromosome shape rather than XY makeup that creates a stronger compulsion within them to commit a crime. This type of person is called a big man. One study found that the number of XYY men in prison was higher than that of men in general; however, some studies do not provide the evidence.

3. William Sheldon Theory

Sheldon believed that humans could be divided into three basic categories, which correspond to three distinct personalities.

- Endomorphic (fat and soft) - are considered soft and fat. They are described as thin, underdeveloped, and round and often have difficulty losing weight. These people are not involved in crime.

- Ectomorphic (thin and fragile) - their body is described as flat, soft, slim, with small shoulders and thin. Furthermore, they are not acquainted with a crime.

- Mesomorphic (muscular and strong) - they are muscular, and their body is described as an hourglass-shaped (female body), or rectangular shape (male body) has a magnificent body, gains muscle quickly, and has firm skin. Mesomorphs, according to Sheldon, are prone to crime.

· **What does addiction does to our brain**

Addiction knocks the brain on many levels, as we can always see that addiction of anything is hazardous on any level. Once the chemical reaches the brain, it can lose control of their impulses or develop a strong desire for a dangerous substance. The brain desires the reward of substance when someone develops an addiction. This is due to the brain's reward system is overstimulated. In response to the continuous use of substances unlocks a host of euphoric feelings and strange behavioural traits. Long term effects can cause brain damage and even result in death.

- **How a human mind is attracted towards drugs** -

- Education has a significant impact on the development of a person's personality; if the person's educational qualification is less and they do not get jobs, they remain unemployed,and more often they are gradually attracted to the people same as them, and they find consuming drugs as the easiest way to deal with stress, anxiety and depression. Moreover, as a result, once they start consuming it, their brain becomes habitual to drugs, and it is a never-ending process.
- Job is another major factor playing a crucial role in drug addiction; when a person is not satisfied with his/her job or is not being paid accordingly, such people deal with stress and depression more and start consuming drugs which further may lead to robbery, lying as an easy way to escape from things.
- Drug addiction makes a person dull and lazy. A drug-addicted person would not like to work, as an average person does. They will be attracted to works like theft, exploitation, murders.
- Moreover, early childhood traumatic experiences like domestic violence within the family, parental neglecting the child, sexual assault, low socio-economic status, lower resources or any other kind of abuse and peer pressure which goes unreported during early or late adolescent years, lack of education can consequently result in individuals resorting to a getaway or escape to deal with their emotions and negative life experiences. Hence just taking a drug once to escape from all these issues takes no time into becoming a shortcut to get away with any issue or difficulty or to release those feel-good hormoneslike serotonin, dopamine, which are called happy hormones, thus creating new brain pathways that reward them every time drug is consumed.
- Often people commit crimes for the first time, which they think are not harmful according to them. For example, picking money from home (can go unnoticed) and this minor crime can turn to significant dangerous crimes and as a way of showing off among their peers. Drug addiction at this stage is increased in terms of showing off, and an easy way of doing

anything develops in the mind of humans.

· Prevention of Crime

The construction of a safe and secure society requires the prevention of crime, which is a necessity for solid economic growth through a continued company investment, as well as community well-being and cohesion. Because it is more cost-effective and leads to more significant societal benefits than traditional approaches to crime, the government must move beyond law enforcement and criminal justice to address the risk factors that generate crime.

· Key elements in crime prevention

- Ways of resolving disputes peacefully have shown their effectiveness.
- A sense of trust between individuals and institutions contributes directly to the success of safety and security actions.
- The active participation of people involved in prevention strategies is a guarantee of success.

· Crime Prevention in India-

Crime prevention is one of the most critical tasks for the Indian police in section 23 of the Police Act of 1861.
- Effective police work
- Monitoring of crime hotspots, foot patrols and mobile surveillance is conducted by the police in crime hotspots. The presence of police in the area itself has the effect of blocking.
- Hue notices and complaints, police issued public awareness and others on the activities of criminals they see. Posters are sometimes published to inform the general public about criminal activity in the area.
- Reduction of property, suspected criminal assets may be seized and lost following the law to prevent offenders from committing crimes by producing goods and property.
- Psychological counselling, counselling is essential to prevent crimes primarily related to family disputes, domestic violence, lobola and civil strife.

- Police investigation and documents - Plays a vital role in crime prevention. It helps to curb criminal desire and threaten organized crime. All police stations keep proper records and properly reviewed them for criminals to keep an eye on them.

- Punishment - Fear of punishment is an old-fashioned way of keeping potential criminals and those who have been imprisoned away from criminal activities. The Indian penal code prescribes preventive punishment for all types of criminals. A criminal expert generally believes that it is not the severity of the punishment but the certainty of the punishment that hinders it. Moreover, with specific penalties, the quality of the investigation should improve. Punishment can be an effective tool in crime prevention programs.

- Social cohesion - Law enforcement agencies cannot work alone. They need the public's cooperation at every step in their work, from collecting information to the investigation of prosecutions to the final reunification of the offenders in the community. Social cohesion is crucial in reducing crime. Without social cohesion, the police cannot function. Social cohesion must be achieved by launching an effective fight against crime and criminals.

- **Crime Prevention Promotes Law Governance and Human Rights-**

Successful crime prevention contributes to law enforcement and human rights. In other words, the opportunity to live a very free life from being a victim of crime is a fundamental human right.

- **Crime Prevention Should be a Holy Part of Economic Development, Politics and Social Development-**

Crime is a significant obstacle to economic, political, and social development. In this way, donor communities and international development partners must incorporate international cooperation in crime prevention in all their efforts to achieve the UN's development goals. International crime prevention cooperation should pay special attention to youth living in poverty and social marginalization.

- **Prevention of Terrorism Requires Proper equipment-**

To implement effective crime prevention, many countries will need specialized guidelines, tools, and other materials.

· Analysis

This paper emphasizes the social impact of crime and ideology, in which a considerable number of criminal ideas are formed through social research. These ideas have highlighted the importance of human diversity, social and cultural perspectives, trying to understand how external social influences can contribute to deviation fully. A Chicago school has learned how places and town planning can affect the development of crime. Complex theorists focus on the acceptance and achievement of goals in society. Social control theory also analyses our social obligations that may allow or prevent deviant behaviour.

The label's view assumes that people listed as deviant will be deviant. Opposing crime experts say that crime results fromthe oppression of power, gender, and equality. Each of these ideas can provide a basis for developing crime prevention and control policies. Social causes of crime certainly demand the prevention of deviations from changes in social and social policy.

Definitions based on biological theories and sensible choices have long been used as a basis for understanding why people commit crimes. As society changes, so do our definitions, but we are far from the end of the universe in what leads people to deviance or crime.

Psychological perspectives focus on the definition of depraved behaviour at each level, such as internal thinking processes or personality traits. People's opinions and psychosis are also presented as definitions of criminal behaviour. The psychological definition of deviation often seeks individual treatment and rehabilitation policies instead of significant social changes.

The causes of deviation are very much related to what we do about it as a society. Policies designed to prevent and reduce deviations are primarily based on what the public believes is the cause of deviation. As we have learned, with new ideas, new policies will follow.

· Conclusion

In the paper, we have given our review of the significant ideas on crime. All of these ideas are still being used, tested, and redesigned by some crime experts. These different perspectives tell us how crime is created in our society that causes harm to everyone in society. These ideas help us to know how each person is involved in crime and how they react in the social environment. Psychological and social perspectives focused on the definitions of immoral behaviour, and all ideas can provide a basis for assisting in the development of crime prevention and control policies. Definitions based on biological factors and sensible choices are often the basis for understanding why a person commits a crime.

Crime prevention will effectively eliminate the source of crime and bring about a peaceful world in which all people will see their potential as individuals and build satisfying and meaningful relationships with others.

· **References**

1. Britannica (2019). Criminology - Major concepts and theories | Britannica. In: *Encyclopædia Britannica*. [online] Available at: https://www.britannica.com/science/criminology/Major-concepts-and-theories

2. Lawrence Kohlberg's Six Stages of Moral Development. (n.d.). *Conclusions*. [online] Available at:https://kohlbergstagesofmoraldevelopment.weebly.com/ conclusions.html#:~:text=Conclusion [Accessed 23 Aug. 2021].

3. Criminal Justice (2015). *Criminal Justice*. [online] Criminal Justice. Available at: http://criminal-justice.iresearchnet.com/criminology/theories/psychological-theories-of-crime/.

4. Umair Aslam (2014). *Biological theory of crime.* [online] Available at: https://www.slideshare.net/umairaslam547389/biological-theory-of crime#:~:text=CRIME%20%EF%82%A7%20Definition%20Behaviour%20that [Accessed 23 Aug. 2021].

5. Criminal Justice. (n.d.). *Strain Theories of Crime (Criminology Theories) IResearchNet.* [online] Available at: https://criminal-justice.iresearchnet.com/criminology/theories/strain-theories/10/.

6. SarrahKaviwala(2017). *Economic Crimes.* [online] Available at: https://www.slideshare.net/SarrahKaviwala/economic-crimes-72969776 [Accessed 23 Aug. 2021].

V

Environment Crime Crises: How To Protect

Authored By: Asst. Prof.Vijayshree Boaddh & Asst. Prof. Veena Chironje Deharia

Govt. Law College Guna M.P., & Govt. JaywantiHaskar P.G. College Betule

· **Abstract**

The research paper is mainly focused on safeguards measures of environmental crime. The main object of this paper is to define protective laws regarding environmental crime. Under the introductory portion, there is define illegal activity conducted by human beings which are directly harmed to the environment that is wildlife crime, illegal fishing, illegal logging and pollution crime. This chapter also included the application of economic theories of criminal law to environmental pollution and their safeguards.

It describesthe effectiveness of environmental criminal law is generally addressed and the consequences of various possible enforcement strategies. It describes environmental degradation and global environmental crimes due to this environmental degradation, Impacts on human beings'lifestyle and what issues are conducted. There are many laws to define how to protect the environment, but the necessity is to execute punishment provisions as well. So the provisions relating to the execution of punishment aredefined in our research paper. In this paper, we also discuss the provisions related to an international level, like provisions given in international conferences and different treaties.Lastly,itdescribed the role of the judiciary to protected environmental crime and critical analysis of environmental laws and suggestions about how to protect environmental crime.

- **Key Words:** -

Sustainable Development, Global Environmental crime, Judicial activism, Environmental degradation, Wildlife crime.

> **"Environment is no one's property to destroy; It is everyone's responsibility to protect."**
> **-By MohithAgadi**

- **Introduction**

At the beginning of human civilization, man has destroyed the environment for fulfilling our basic needs, such as flooding, cultivation, fishing, timber for cooking food. This situation was continuously run-up to many centuries but in 14th to 15th centuries world mechanism are move to developing of infrastructure in countries. As a result, it generates a problem of crime against the environment and wildlife. These mechanisms of development are cause damage to the environment and wildlife around us.

In the world scenario, they are considered as a category under the organized criminal activities. It is taken the fourth most significant area of crime in the list of organized crime in the world. These types of crimes are also called green-collar crimes.

There is various type of crime included Under green-collar crimes such as Poaching, illegal Trade of wildlife, Trade of unregulated or illegal product for financial and material gains. Hence, to stop this type of activity in Stockholm first conference was held in 1972 for the protection of the environment. (S.R. Myneni, 2013) Similar situations Earth-summit, Agenda-21, Reo-conference are held.

Indian status-At Present, there are many laws to protect the environment in India like Environmental Protection Law 1986, Air and water protection Law. (S.C. Tripathi, 2005),However, due to no penal provision in the laws but the laws are continuously violated by the people due to which environmental crimes are increasing. Incorporating penal provisions in environmental legislation is necessary to reduce the increasing environmental offences.

· Research Methodology

For the present research paper, the researcher has adopted both Doctrinal and non-Doctrinal research, but mainly non-Doctrinal research or experience-based research has been used by the researcher, as well as the research created by the researcher through a case study.

The research has been done by the researcher based on his experience or observation, who has tried to verify his hypothesis from the study material collected through observation and case study. The purpose of conducting non-Doctrinal research by the researcher is closer to originality and judicial decisions also prove to be very useful in empirical research. Theoretical research has also been used by the researcher in the said research paper. That is, secondary sources have been used by the researcher for theoretical research.

· Statement of Problem

Over the past decades, the international agencies have playeda significant role in codifying laws related to environmental protection; their examples are the Stockholm conference, Earth conference. (A.Usha, 2007). Although by international efforts, India has also made legal provisions for environmental protection and then in 1986, the Environment Protection Act 1986 was passed.

The laws in India for environmental protection are not enough because there is no penal provision anywhere in those laws. Due to the absence of penal provisions, there is a continuous violation of these laws, which shows the inadequacy of these laws. The main problem before the researcher is to protect the legislation related to the environment so that environmental crime can be stopped. To prevent the environment, penal provisions should be included in the environmental legislation so that the justification of the environmental legislation remains and the environment can be protected.

A problem before the researcher is also to establish a balance between environmental protection and development. All the countries are moving towards development, so environmental crimes are increasing continuously, but the methods for environmental protection are insufficient because there is a lack of penal provisions.

· **Review of literature**

After independence, many important laws related to the environment have been made in the Indian Constitution; the most critical step in this was the 40th constitutional amendment of the supreme legislation. By this, the provisions related to environmental protection were included in Article 48 (A), after which, by the 42nd Constitutional Amendment, the duty was imposed on the citizens in Article 51 (A) that they would protect the environment.

If we talk about special laws, then there are Environmental Protection Law 1986, Water Pollution Law 1974, and Air Pollution Law 1981 related to the environment; the primary purpose of the laws related to environmental protection is to protect and improve the environment. (S.C. Tripathi, 2005) Apart from this, to implement the decision of the Stockholm Convention, to protect human beings, animals, and plants from hazards, to enact a general and comprehensive law for environmental protection, to create authorities for environmental protection, to those who threaten human-environmental safety and health. The primary purpose of the above laws was to provide for preventive punishment.

These methods have been successful in their purpose to some extent, but even today, the purpose of the system of punishment could not be fulfilled, due to which environmental crimes are increasing, and we are continuously increasing the need for laws, and there is also a need for such methods which were in the past. protect the laws made.

Under the environmental legislation, all the powers have been centralized in the central Government, which is not necessary; despite forest maintenance being the most important subject, there is no provision in the environmental legislation, not only this but in case of damage due to pollution, a private suit is filed for damages. There is a lack of provision to do so.

The High Court and Supreme Courts have taken a progressive approach under the writ jurisdiction in protecting the environment. Courts have also played an essential role in protecting the environment through public interest litigation and have guided for environmental protection through various litigations(Areti Krishna Kumari, 2007) such as-

· **Rural Litigation and Entitlement Center Dehradun[1], the Court has propounded the principle that-**

i. Environment and Any kind of business cannot be allowed at the cost of ecological balance
ii. There is a conflict between development and environment and ecology, there must be harmony between the two.(J.J.R.Upadhya, 2016)

Similarly, guidelines were given in other important cases, but there is still a lack of penal provisions in the laws.

· **Research Questions: -**

The following questions have been created by the researcher in the said research paper-

i. Are there any methods to balance development and environmental protection?
ii. Are there enough laws for increasing environmental crime?
iii. Whether the environmental law is currently protected, or is it being violated continuously?
iv. Whether it is necessary to provide punitive to preserve environmental law?

· **The objective of the research: -**

The purpose of the researcher in the research paper is not only to suggest measures to prevent environmental crime from happening in the Present, as well as to present suggestions to preserve the methods which are there in the past for environmental protection.

The researcher's objective is to suggest measures to harmonize environmental protection and development. All the nations are moving towards development, so they are constantly harming the environment in some way or the other, so the researcher aims to suggest measures to prevent environmental crime at the international level.

· **Judicial activism in the development of environmental legislation**

The Court's primary function is to interpret the existing law and formulate rights and duties between the parties concerned. In the backdrop of the emergence of environmental law and international commitment in the last three decades and the new interpretation of Article 21 given in the case of **Smt. Maneka Gandhi v. Union of India[2]**, the Supreme Court has emphasised public interest litigation to protect the environment. Be sure to start. In order to protect the environment, the Supreme Court resorted to progressive elections and tried to implement them effectively by ignoring their enforceable nature to make the Directive Principles of State Policy and Fundamental Duties meaningful. All these steps have been possible only because of judicial creativity. (Aniruddh Prasad, 2018)

The Court tried to fill the administrative void by taking over administrative activities and resorted to judicial activism to fill the void created by the farewell inaction. Not only this, but the Court also converted the centuries-old *"Principle of strict liability"* as *"principle of Absolute liability"* in the context of the industrial revolution in the new angel crisis. The Supreme Court, through the principle of *"polluter, pays"*, not only compensated the people who were hurt by pollution on the polluter but also passed an order to repair the damage caused to the environment itself. The Supreme Court issued directions to the Central Government, State Governments and Central Pollution Boards and State Pollution Boards and various municipal corporations intending to give effect to the principle of prior caution. Cases of judicial mobility include cases propounding the principle of unlimited liability, cases implementing the principles of prior due diligence and polluters pay the principles, monitoring, giving directions for setting up of green bench and environment protection fund. Departing from tradition, judicial innovation has been initiated.

· *Principle of Absolute Liability–*

TheEmergenceSupreme Court propounded the *principle of Absolute liability* by adopting a new revolutionary approach regarding the liability of hazardous and hazardous industries.(S.Shanthakumars, 2016) The Supreme Court rejected the principle of strict liability as propounded in the centuries-old **Rylands vs flecther[3]** and applied the principle of absolute liability.

The Supreme Court said that-

"We are of the view that an enterprise which is blood in peril or an inherently hazardous industry, which is beneficial to the health of the people working in the industry and the people in the immediate neighbourhood. Furthermore, may effectively endanger safety, he assumes a full and non-plan duty to the community to ensure that the angel conducted by him is in danger or caused by the activity of an inherently dangerous nature."

The Court held them that-

"An enterprise must be deemed to be liable to conduct the hazardous or inherently dangerous activity with the highest standards of safety and if such activity results in any loss, the enterprise shall and no reply will be acceptable on the part of the enterprise that it had exercised reasonable care and caused damages without negligence on its part".

- ***Polluter pays principle and principle of due diligence-***

The promulgation of the Pollutants Pay principle is a part of rudimentary international law, but the Supreme Court of India has applied it in tannery cases by introducing judicial activity. (Aniruddh Prasad, 2018).

The Supreme Court has expressed that the *"principle of due diligence"* and *"the polluter pays principle"* are essential characteristics of sustainable development. Where did the polluter pay principle go in explaining that entire liability for environmental damage includes not only paying compensation to the victims of pollution but also the cost of correcting environmental damage? (I.A.Khan, 2002) Damage treatment is part of a sustainable development process that requires payment for repairing individual victims and ecological damage.

- **Propounded Principles-**

i. Precautionary Doctrine and Pollutants Pay Principle are accepted as the law of the land Article 21, 48A and 51A (g) and Environment Protection Act are the means of implementing these principles.

ii. Rudigenous international law shall, if not inconsistent with the law of the country, be deemed to be subsumed into domestic or civil law.

iii. An "environmental protection method" can be established to implement the polluter effectively pays principle.

iv. In the event of failure on the part of the Government to constitute regulatory/decisive statutory officers, it is for the Court to pass appropriate necessary directions.

v. High Court specific "Green Bench" can be constituted to deal with the matters related to environmental law.(Anriuddh Prasad, 2018)

· ***Principle of Public Credit for Ecological Protection-***

The Supreme Court, while applying the principle of *"Public Credit"*in environmental matters, clarified that people have the right to expect that certain lands and natural areas will maintain their natural characteristics. The people developed by the Roman Empire is based on the core principle that specific resources such as air, sea, water and forests are essential to people, that making them subjects of private ownership would be Annapurna. Resources are the gift of nature and should be made readily available to every person in this life without any attention from the applicant. The High Court, like American courts, accepted this principle to distribute water to rivers and lands important to ecology; the Court clarified that it is part of our jurisprudence. All resources are required by nature to be used and consumed by the public. Seacoasts are the fathers of water, air and ecologically soft land. Protect natural resources that are required for use and cannot be converted into private ownership.

Based on the principle of the Court, three restrictions on the power of the state were hunted-

i. Trust property should not be used only for public purposes but should be held to make it available for ordinary people.
ii. The property cannot be sold even if it has a fair cash value.
iii. Property should be held for specific types of uses.(Anriuddh Prasad, 2018)

The Supreme Court made it clear that in the absence of a legislative act, the people cannot convert them into private ownership or commercial use by absolving them of their obligations regarding natural resources due to the principle of cooperation. The aesthetic sense and new dignity of natural resources cannot be subjected to private or commercial use.

The environmental laws have failed to fulfil the intended purpose due to a lack of enforcement process and neglect of officials. The Court can give directions, but it cannot be a substitute for administrative officers. Therefore, there is a need that the information related to environmental impact assessment should be widely disseminated, the government organizations should be made more active, and the general public should be made aware by informing about the dangers arising out of environmental pollution so that they can choose to solve the environmental problem. To put pressure on the bodies and officials.

The role of the judiciary in reconciling between development and environmental protection: -

The environment is not only a problem of developed countries, but it is also a problem of developing countries, and development is an important problem of developing countries. Since India is a developing country and due to increasing industrialization, environmental problems are increasing continuously. The Court has an important role to play in bringing about harmony between development and the environment. The development of the country is necessary, and at the same time, it is also the responsibility of the Government to protect the human right to a clean environment, which is our fundamental right, so the damage caused to the environment by the industrial establishment also violates our fundamental right, hence environmental protection. Moreover, in order to harmonize the development, the Supreme Court has presented a guide through various cases.

- **Tehri Dam case[4]-**

This case is related to environmental aspect and safety, in this case, the judges gave their opinion that-

i. The balance between environmental protection and development works is possible only by strict adherence to the principles of sustainable development;a sustainable development environment Ensures development while preserving Sustainable development works for all people and all generations. It is a guarantee of the Present and a will of the future.
ii. The right to a clean environment is our fundamental right.
iii. Ensuring sustainable development is one of the objectives of the Environment Law 1986.(Aniruddh Prasad, 2018)

Indeed, through the suit, the Court created the concept of sustainable development. Sustainable development is a vital link to establish a balance between environmental protection and development.

- **Narmada Bachao case[5]-**

After the above said, many problems, including rehabilitation of people affected by dam construction and the environment started arising, while giving judgment in the ratio of 3:2 in this case, Judge B.N. Kripal said that-

i. The water requirement of the increasing population For this, the construction of the Sardar Sarovar Dam is in the public interest.
ii. Displacement of people due to dam construction will not be considered a violation of fundamental rights.
iii. Damage caused to the environment by constructinga dam can be compensated by planting a forest on another land.
iv. A mere change in environmental conditions cannot be assumed that the construction of a dam will lead to ecological disaster.

But Judge Bharucha gave his decision disproportionately and said that-

i. The clearance given in the absence of data on environmental impact cannot be considered correct.
ii. If the plan is not completed, there should be an option that the displaced people can return to their former place provided that place remains habitable.
iii. Public interest litigation should not be dismissed merely on the ground of inordinate delay.(Aniruddh Prasad, 2018)

In both the above cases, a guide was provided by the Court for environmental protection, but if the condition of forestation is not fulfilled, then the penal provisions have not been mentioned in the decision, as a result of which the damage to the environment has been compensated till date was not done. The main reason for this is the absence of penal provisions in our environmental law.

- **Environmental Crime and legitimacy of law: -**

Environmental law has not been defined the environmental crime anywhere environmental protection, and it has gone to provide power to the central Government in environmental legislation to improve but if any person or entity environmental Humor If he does, there is still a lack of legislation to punish him. Measures have been suggested for environmental protection by the guidelines obtained through the decisions of the courts. However, there is no punitive legislation for the protection of the measures, due to which they are being violated continuously because of environmental protection law and justify power has continued to decline.

Environmental crimes are increasing continuously; there are many reasons for this, such as population abundance and continuous increase in it, competition for industrial development and misuse of resources, urbanization, highly technical reasons and development of scientific technology, excessive use of energy, unplanned development, unlimited mining, natural Destruction of flora and fauna.

The ever-increasing population is putting a burden on natural resources. In order to meet the convenience of the growing population, nature is being mistreated due to industrialization, the use of heavy machinery and chemicals is increasing, and industrial progress is being considered necessary for economic development and social progress. Industrial development is becoming the benchmark of modernity. Due to industrial development, the environment is being damaged, due to which environmental crimes are increasing continuously, this work is continuously harming the country like slow poison, and due to which the environment is gradually being destroyed, similarly due to urbanization, the trees around the city Unplanned development of river valley project is also becoming a cause of the environmental crisis. Similarly, human beings knowingly or unknowingly are committing crimes against the environment continuously, but there is no penal provision for crimes in the environmental law.

Under the environmental protection law, the Central Government has been empowered to protect and improve the environment; the Government passed the National Green Tribunal Act in 2010 to protect the environment. This law was passed for environmental protection, protection of any legal right including forest protection environment and protection of other natural resources and relief and compensation for the damage caused to the people and property. It also aims at effective and speedy disposal of issues related to environmental protection.

Under this method, if anyone fails to comply with the order or the Panchat or the decision, he will be punished with imprisonment of up to 3 years or with ? 100000000 or both. The biggest drawback of this method is that if someone causes damage to the environment, no other person would spend his time and money and bring a suit in the Court for environmental protection. This Tribunal also suo-moto does not bring any guidance or suit so that the environment is protected. If all the people keep ignoring environmental protection, then surely there will be no justification for such tribunals and environmental protection laws. The greatest need is to protect the laws related to the environment.

- **Critical Analysis**

Efforts have been made not only at the national level but also at the international level to preserve the environment. It is the result of efforts at the international level that today there are many methods for environmental protection in India.

This law makes provisions for environmental protection, but its biggest drawback is that if anyone violates this law, then there is a lack of penal provisions for it. It lacks methods to preserve the environmental protection method. To fill this gap, in the year 2010, the Government of India passed another law, the National Green Tribunal Act, 2010. (Aniruddh Prasad, 2018) Although there is a penal provision in this Tribunal, the vital drawback of this tribunal is that it has not met the criterion of speedy disposal, due to which the number of cases pending before the Tribunal is increasing, some examples of this are as follows-

i. In Tamnar of Chhattisgarh, the power plant case lay more than two years for.
ii. The matter of work pollution from coal mine activities and thermal power plant of Singrauli district went before the Tribunal from September 2013, which remained pending for years.
iii. The matter of non-acceptance of coal quality by Maharashtra State Power Generation Company remained before the National Green Tribunal without any definite order.

- Another drawback of Tribunal is-

i. That there are only five green tribunal benches in the whole of India which are out of reach of the general public, and hence it is not accessible to the general public.

ii. It can also be criticized for the formation of the Green Tribunal, being a judicial person in the National Green Tribunal, the views of the technical expert are not considered, for example, an expert with experience in the forest department for a long time, to deal with the issues arising from industrial pollution will not be able to understand.

iii. Although the power of the Tribunal to take suo-moto cognizance is not explicitly mentioned in the law, but the Green Tribunal can initiate suo-moto proceedings under the broad powers in the law. However, despite having the power, the National Green Tribunal is indifferent in the matter of protecting the environment. (Aniruddh Prasad, 2018)

The laws for which environmental protection have been made for, there is a need to protect those laws so that they cannot be violated, and their justification remains.

· Conclusion and Recommendation

To protect the environment, the most important thing is that from the most minor punishment to the significant punishment, provisions should be made. An explicit provision should be made in the Act to suo-moto an institution like National Green Tribunal.

Conservation of environmental law at the international level requires that the principle of sustainable development be followed. There should be an obligation to comply with the principles that have been brought from the conferences held at the international level; the nation which does not obey these rules should be excommunicated from the member of the United Nations. Do not cooperate with such a nation as a punishment to understand the importance of the environment.

In addition to this, the following suggestions are presented to protect the environment and to protect the laws related to it-

i. The nations should receive the annual report to ensure that the rules are made by organizing conferences every year to protect the environment at the international level.

ii. If the environment is polluted more than the standard level by any nation, then it should be directed to the plantation, and if that nation does not follow it, then there should be the provision of penal provisions for the exclusion of the nations.

iii. All nations should be directed to make provisions to include environmental protection laws in their national laws.

iv. Penal provisions should be included more and more for environmental protection, and there should be many types of these penal provisions.

v. Institutions like the National Green Authority for Environment Protection should be established in all the districts so that the claims can be settled at the earliest.

vi. It is the responsibility of all persons to protect their environment, but if they are causing damage or seeing the environment around them causing damage, they should impose the duty of suing the Tribunal.

vii. The laws which are made for environmental protection should be reformed, and provision of various types of penal provisions should be made.

viii. Development work should be done only by establishing a balance between environmental protection and development.

ix. The concept of sustainable development should be strictly followed.

x. Environment-related methods should be included in school education so that all children can become aware of environmental protection and provide a clean environment for their coming generation.

If we follow the above suggestions, then undoubtedly our environment will be protected. Only then the purpose of environmental law will also be successful and environmental law will be protected only when we will discharge our duties successfully by following the above suggestions.

- **References**

1. A.I.R. 1985 S.C. 652
2. A.I.R. 1978 S.C. 587
3. (1868) L.R. 3 H.L. 330.
4. S.C.C. (2004)9, 362
5. A.I.R. 2000 S.C. 3751
6. Khan, I.A.(2002). Environmental Law. Edition-Second.Allahabad: Central Law Agency, Page(255).
7. Tripathi, S.C.(2005). Environmental Law. Edition-Second.Allahabad: Central Law Publications, Page(449).
8. Shanthakumars, S.(2016). Introduction to Environmental Law. Edition-Second. South Africa: LexisNexis, Page(101)

9. Kumari, A. Krishna (2007). Environmental Jurisprudence. Hyderabad: The ICFAI University Press, Page(218)

10. Usha, A. (2007). Environmental Law Principles and Governance. Hyderabad: The ICFAI University Press, Page(14-15)

11. Rural Litigation and Entitlement Center Dehradun vs. State of U.P.,(1985) S.C. 652(India)

12. Smt. Maneka Gandhi vs. Union of India,(1978) S.C. 587(India)

13. Rylands vs. flecther,(1868)3 S.C. 330(India)

14. N.D.Jayal vs. Union of India, (2004)9 S.C.362(India)

15. Narmada BachaoAandolan vs. Union of India,(2000) S.C. 3751(India)

VI

The Institution of Marriage and National Integration

Authored By: Yash Choudhary

Student, Law Centre - I, Faculty of Law, University of Delhi)

· **Abstract**

Marriage is an ancient institution existing in almost every society around the world. Two individuals come together to form the union of marriage, which gives rise to a family, which further forms the society, which ultimately forms the nation. Thus, the institution of marriage can be said to be the very foundation block of a nation. Being the foundation block, it could be used to integrate the masses by eliminating the differences. Little steps have been taken in this direction by the legislature and socio-religious institutions. This paper aims to discuss how this institution could integrate different sections into a nation, the various challenges involved and possible solutions. Since religious and communal conflicts are on the rise in present times in India, it seems to be the right time to explore this dimension.

· **Keywords:** *Marriage, national integration, inter-religious, inter-caste, inter-state, inter-faith*

- **Introduction**

Uttar Pradesh prohibition of unlawful religious conversion ordinance, 2020, popularly known as the "lovejihad law ", seeks to prevent religious conversion by 'allurement'. This law has sparked much controversy among advocates, jurists. Because it uses the word 'allurement', which has a broad connotation, for example, even giving a religious book to a person can amount to allurement. Several jurists believe that the law would make inter-faith marriages difficult. This is so because the religious conversions for marriage in Uttar Pradesh under the act must be approved by the district magistrate.

An effect of this provision would be that it would lead to an increase,i.e., religious separatism in an atmosphere when communal violence and religious sectarian conflicts are on the risen of the country. For example, when the Centre passed the Citizenship (Amendment) Act, it triggered mass protests in different parts of the country, with violent incidents, especially in the national capital. Now, such provisions as the said 'love jihad law' seem to give strength to individual religious identities by defining the boundaries of religion, posing a threat to the amalgamation of religious identities. This could lead to an increase in religious extremism. Another effect of this law could be that it might lead to the suppression of women as it seems to impose restrictions on a woman's choice of her life partner. Moreover, the punishment in case the victim of allurement is S.C., S.T., women, is 10years imprisonment, which is five years otherwise. So, it treats women to be historically marginalized.

The Indian society remains a deeply divided society, even after seventy-four years of independence, evident from communal riots such as the Muzaffarnagar riots (2013) and the CAA protests, which resulted in communal violence(2020). In this background comes a law that affects the role of religion in the institution of marriage. So, considering the prevailing conditions, it becomes essential to study national integration, the problems faced in the process and how marriage as an institution could be used to bring together a society that is falling apart.

- **Research methodology**

The research dwells into various dimensions of national integration and different ways in which marriage influences society. It also highlights the contemporary developments in the society and decisions of the judiciary and attempts to find solutions for different challenges involved. The research methodology adopted is socio-legal.

· Marriage and Its Role in Society

Marriage has always been a fundamental institution in the eyes of society, and every society has been defining marriage and rituals according to the social needs of the people of that society. Marriage is a strong union. Every society, whatever be the religion, fundamentally looked at marriage in this same way. For example, Hinduism talks about marriage as an indissoluble union, Islam talks about marriage as a firm contract, Christian view of marriage is describing as in between a man and a woman and that it is solemn and public covenant in the presence of God.

On careful observation of societies across the world, one finds out that marriage has existed in almost every society across the world. So, it must have had great importance in the eyes of people and religious leaders across the world. If one comes to the social aspect of marriage, its importance lies in the fact that it leads to the creation of a family, which creates a society that further goes on to create the nation. An individual decides to involve himself in society primarily because he has some vested interest, his personal or of his family's, which he might see being fulfilled by the society. So, it can be said that marriage is the keystone of the monument called nation.

The importance of marriage as an institution can also be recognized by the fact that the so-called"open western society" such as the USA, where the systems of the old order are continuously questioned based on rationality, have not yet been able to dissolve this institution, probably because it gives some sense of security and legal protection to the people involved. Also, marriage has always been considered necessary for the spiritual uplift of an individual because it initiates a process of dissolution of one's sense of identity, thereby reducing the emotions of arrogance and jealousy in an individual, which in turn enables them to work for larger good as they can associate themselves with other beings.

So, based on this study, it may be determined that to give a proper direction to society, it is essential to have a legal system that governs the coming together of two individuals. The Indian society has lately seen the growing influence of Western cultures, which promote live-in relationships and open marriages. This can be anenormous problem as such relationships might cause the people to be driven by their personal needs, biological, physical, emotional. If this happens in society, then people would

Not work in a cooperative manner or for achieving a larger goal because their own life would not be settled, and this would drive the society haywire, as can be seen in the present state of the American society where drug abuse, sexual exploitation of women, mental health issues are on the rise.

· **National integration**

According to Myron Weiner, "national integration implies avoidance of divisive movements that would balkanize the nation and presence of attitudes throughout the society that give preference to national and public interests as distinct from parochial interests. (Myron Weiner, 1963)".

According to H. A.Gani, "national integration is a socio-psychological and educational process through which a feeling of unity, solidarity and cohesion develops in the hearts of the people and a sense of common citizenship or feeling of loyalty to the nation is fostered among them(Myron Weiner, 1963)."

One can say that national integration involves several dimensions such as political, economic, psychological, cultural, social, religious. National integration of India since independence has been facing several problems such as regional differences, religious differences, caste-based discrimination that continues to exist all these years among the people. To ultimately achieve the goal of national integration, it is essential to find a solution that would address all the problems and needs of the present circumstances.

· Such a solution should have the following two characteristics:

(1) the solution should be progressive, capable of changing with the changing needs of the society.

(2) the solution should be accommodative, i.e., it should include and consider the interests of all the sections of the society so that none of them feels left out. There should be an effort of creating an environment of acceptance, rather than a mere show of tolerance, by the majority, towards the minority, on moral grounds.

· Marriage as a tool for national integration

Several facets of individual human existence have to be brought together in order to unite them for the creation of a nation. As discussed earlier, several individual interests are involved even in the creation of a society. So, in order to use marriage as a tool for integration, it is essential to look as to how it is capable of bringing about social, economic, political and psychological integration of people.

· Economic integration of masses by marriage –

Every individual has specific economic interests, which multiply with more responsibilities after marriage, e.g., better living standards, education of children. These individual interests lead to the growth of the economic interests of society and, ultimately, the nation.

Marriage can be advantageous in the economic integration of the nation. One of the primary challenges in national integration is regionalism among the people, where an individual's region takes the form of a strong identity within him, which in turn brings about a lot of conflicts. In the post-1991 liberalization of India, communal differences and disturbances have been on the rise. One of the reasons is that, as private sector investment increased in India, the domestic handloom and embroidery industry was struck. These small industries had primarily been controlled by Muslims, and they suffered a loss of income; and due to the lack of a proper education system in the society, they were rendered unemployable. If in this condition, the society encourages marriages between individuals belonging to different regions, then this could certainly be a solution.

A consequence of such marriages could be that they would sync with the growing culture of destination weddings, wherein the boy and the girl, belonging to different regions and cultures, would choose to marry at a common location. Thiscould be a boom in the tourism industry as some states, due to their geographical location, would be having an advantage as organizers of the destination weddings. Furthermore, if this starts happening on a large scale, India could also become a "popular wedding avenue", attracting couples from other countries to conduct wedding ceremonies in India. Now, this would undoubtedly lead to an increase in the movement of economic resources into the areas which can become desirable destinations. When economic resources move from one state to another, this could be a positive sign for economic integration. There are already examples of foreigners attracted by the Indian culture and wedding rituals coming to India to get married in Indian style.

If such large-scale weddings are encouraged in India, then this opportunity could be used to promote the domestic handloom and embroidery industry by promoting domestically produced fabrics such as Kanjeevaram and Patola saris. This way, the government could promote the domestic industry and subsequently organize the workers involved into a cooperative society which would lead to a decrease in unemployment rates and enhance the sense of cooperation in the people of society.

Another step that the society can take could be encouraging the Indian culture of "Dana" or voluntary donation of money or resources to the poorer sections of the society. This culture had existed since ancient times in order to keep the movement of wealth going from one section of society to the other. In present times, it could be used in a marriage where the bride and the bridegroom could donate a certain amount of money to the poorer section of society, thereby maintaining the economic balance.

During personal analysis of the writer in Gujarani village of District Bhiwani in Haryana, it was found that around 10% of agricultural labourers were married in a different state. Some of them, who are married into families with no sons, were found to be helping their wives' families with their agricultural activities. So, if marriages are promoted between different regions, then this could also lead to boosting of the agricultural economy, which would be a significant step in the integration of nation economically.

- **Political integration of masses by marriage –**

Political integration, in simple words, could be defined as the shifting of loyalties by the individuals from their religion, region to a larger purpose, which would lead to an integration of communities into a nation. A nation, in turn, being a representative unit of all those individuals and their interests, must have some underlying ideology that represents all the individuals and communities.

The American experience with integration has happened through, among other processes, marriage (exogamy) across ethnic (if not racial), sectarian, religious and regional lines. On the contrary, Pakistan has faced the problem of unintegrated provinces due to the large Muslim population (nearly 98%), which encourages endogamy.

The political integration in the Indian case requires a two-pronged approach, which involves the masses and the political leaders. If people promote marriage in different states, then there would be a migration of people from one state to the other. As a result, there would be an amalgamation of people coming from different regions, and this would help integrate the states as one state would have vested interests in the other due to the presence of their people in that state.

For example, a decision such as the closure of the border between Delhi and Haryana by the Delhi government does not seem practical unless dire circumstances require such a decision. The primary reason being a large chunk of Haryana's population works in Delhi, and a large chunk of Delhi's population works in Gurgaon, which is the city of Haryana. So, such migration of people from one state to other can help resolve interstate disputes and promote better interstate relations.

Another underlying problem of India as a country has been the caste based and religion based differences. These have existed primarily due to the divisive politics of political leaders, where they used communal agendas to garner votes and support. So, in present times the political leaders could help in the process of political integration of India by showing a strong will. They can do so by promoting interfaith or inter-caste marriages of their children or family members. The notion may not be entirely new for Indian society because it has always existed. For example, the Mughal rulers used the policy of "matrimonial alliance "in order to integrate their empire into a unit, where the rulers themselves married girls from a different religion. Not just Mughals, but this policy existed even in the Marathas, Jat rulers, Sikh rulers. So, the moment's need is to re-formulate this policy in a modified format that is suitable for current circumstances.

The political leaders might be sceptical in adopting this stance, but if they do so, then there is an excellent chance that the institution of caste would get diluted, which would lead to the shift of election issues from communal agenda to a developmental agenda by attracting the youth. According to Theodore P. Wright Jr., "Shujra (family trees) of up to 100 leading families obtained during the author's stay in Karachi as a Fulbright grantee in 1983-84 confirm the impression gained previously from a study of the Tyabji clan of SulaimaniBohras in Bombay and of a dozen leading North Indian Muslim clans, almost all of whom have members in Pakistan, that arranged matches outside the family, biradari and linguistic province have long been used by elite lineages to cement political alliances(Theodore P. Wright Jr.,

1994)."

- **Social integration of masses by marriage –**

Social integration of masses refers to integrating individuals in the society by eliminating social evils and creating an atmosphere of acceptance, where individuals discard communal identities. For this process to commence in Indian society, we must undertake two reforms,i.e., dilution of caste as an institution and empowerment of women. The issues of women and caste oppression are interrelated.

Dr. BR Ambedkar had once remarked that the caste system is responsible for the suppression of women. In earlier times, the custom of "Swayamvara "was prevalent in the Indian Society, certain inferences of which can be drawn from ancient stories such as the Ramayana and the Mahabharata, which are reflections of the societies of the time at which they were written. Under this practice, the bride was empowered to choose her groom. Such practices need promotion in present times when women are becoming more independent. This would lead to women's empowerment as decision-makers, and when they exercise their choice freely, they will choose grooms from other castes, which would dilute the institution of caste. Society can promote the idea of "Gandharva marriage", which was prevalent in the earlier times, a classic example being the love story of Shakuntala and Dushyant.

In recent times, however, there has been a changing trend in society. In 2014, the Satrolkhap, which has jurisdiction over 42 villages in the Hisar district of Haryana, allowed inter-caste marriages, which is a big move in eliminating the 600-year-old Norm, which had been extensively promoted by the khap panchayats, inviting much criticism. With the coming of corporate culture and industrialization, women are stepping out of the boundaries of their homes. So, there could be complex with the present needs of society to confine them. Hence, the institution of marriage could be used as a tool to empower women by allowing them to exercise their own choice in marriage and, at the same time, eliminate the evils of casteism.

In Shakti Vahini v. Union of India,[1] the Supreme Court opined, "....It should be borne in mind that when two adults agree unanimously as life partners, it reflects their choice recognized under Sections 19 and 21 of the Constitution. Such a right has the constitutional right, and once it is respected, that right is required to be protected" A few days later, the same bench, in the most specific terms, reiterated this right. In Shafin Jahan v. Asokan K.M and others[2], Article 16 of the Universal Declaration of Human Rights and the Puttaswamy case[3]. The majority held, "The right to marry a person of her choice is part of Article 21of the Constitution of India. Conservative guarantees the right to life. This privilege may not be asserted in the case of prosecutions originating from non-political offences or conduct that are detrimental to the United Nations' goals and objectives. The fundamental freedoms enshrined in the Constitution as a fundamental right are the individual's ability to make important decisions in the pursuit of happiness."

So, the institution of marriage could be used to eliminate the social differences, caste-based and gender-based, in Indian society. Moreover, when these differences get eliminated, one might also see, in future, Inter-caste arranged marriages. Another effect may be the balancing of sex ratio between the states; for example, the states such as Kerala with a surplus of a female child (positive sex ratio) could help create a balance with female deficit state (negative sex ratio) such as Haryana. This could help bring people together and integrate different communities and units in India socially.

- **Psychological integration of masses by marriage –**

Psychological integration can be achieved only by directly affecting and changing the thought process of an individual or individuals at large. The other aspects of national integration could very much help change people's mindset, which could aid psychological integration. Marriage should be viewed as sharing culture and ideas, and the people at large must understand that diversity is the essence of a vibrant society. Inter-regional or inter-religion, or inter-caste marriages would bring with them a combination of people coming from different cultures.

The main problem is that people from one culture view another culture with suspicion and doubt. However, the case of marriage takes the place of a boy with a girl coming from different culture into the household. The family members must allow her to practice her religion and culture. Instead of viewing this with suspicion, they may view this as an opportunity for personal growth where they may learn about practices of a different culture, which may lead to enrichment of their being. It is also very essential that the individuals marrying use the process of mediation with their families and understand their reasons as the parents. Often tend to have some social pressures regarding the marriage of their children. The goal should not be to create an environment of tolerance but to create an environment of acceptance.

A similar social message was given by a Bollywood movie named "two states ", where the families of the boy and the girl were utterly opposed to their wedding as they came from different regions and cultures but eventually, both of them worked together and changed the mindset of their families who at last approved for their marriage. Such movies portray the changing mindset of society. Examples may be cited from medieval Indian history. Akbar, having married Rajput princesses, instead of imposing his religion and cultural practices on his wives, allowed them to practice their religion and even made temples to allow the women to worship their deities, which shows a shift in psychology.

Another exciting fact surfaced during the writer's survey conducted in village Gujrani of District Bhiwani in Haryana. Out of around 3500 people (62% married) surveyed, there were only 5 cases Of marriage by choice; the rest all were cases of arranged marriages. Even in the cases of love marriage, none of them was found to be Inter-caste. There was only one case of inter-religion marriage between a Hindu boy and a Christian girl, which is entirely unacceptable for the villagers and his family members, as a result of which the villagers have wholly sidelined the person in the village community.

However, there were around 50 cases where a woman was from outside Haryana, and some of them were interviewed by the writer. He found that none of them faced any problem in mingling with the village folks. Though there had been some language barriers initially, they were still completely acceptable by the village society. This shows that there are lesser regional disparities as compared to caste and religion-based differences.

- **Law, marriage and national integration**

The existence of different personal laws for Hindus and Muslims has led to the creation of differences in society because of the existence of different sets of laws cabinets different sections of the society into different classifications. These different laws have existed since the British era, as Britishers wanted to create communal differences between the Indian masses.

In order to achieve their purpose, the Britishers followed the policy of divide and rule and used a different set of personal laws to create differences between Hindus and Muslims. In the present era, when India has its Constitution, it should try to propagate the values of secularism and fraternity, which have been enshrined in its preamble itself. The Supreme Court has held the "right to choose one's life partner" to be a right under the ambit of "right to life and personal liberty" enshrined in article 21 of the Constitution in the judgement of "Shakti Vahini V. Union of India"[4].In "Noori Begum v. Senior Superintending of Police Udham Singh Nagar",[5] Uttarakhand High Court observed, "To Choose their life partners is a fundamental right of an adult" and directed the police to protect an inter-faith couple facing family opposition to their union. These decisions show the progressive approach of the judiciary and the gradual change that society is undergoing concerning the institution of marriage.

These decisions show the progressive approach of the judiciary and the gradual change that society is undergoing concerning the institution of marriage.

Article 44 of the Indian Constitution states that "the State shall endeavour to secure for the citizens a uniform civil code (UCC) throughout the territory of India." The institution of marriage can prove to be instrumental in the integration of India if the legal system can achieve the idea of a uniform civil code enshrined in article 44 of the Constitution, as all other institutions of society such as succession, adoption emanate from the institution of marriage itself. In order to achieve the uniform civil code, a significant step had been the non-recognition of gotra and caste under the Hindu marriage act, 1955.

After the Centre revoked Article 370, all of the family law Acts extended to the state of Jammu and Kashmir. Although this is an excellent step towards the implementation of UCC throughout India, still, a long distance is to be covered. If a uniform civil code is enacted, all personal laws will cease to exist. It will do away with gender biases in Muslim, Hindu and Christian law that women have often challenged on the ground that they are violative of the right to equality. So it can prove to be a step towards gender justice, which can be instrumental in integration, as explained earlier.

However, some learnings can be drawn from the Goa civil code, and a similar model could be applied to India to integrate the nation. Regarding the institution of marriage, the registration of every marriage should be made mandatory by every state. The particular marriage act, 1954, should be strengthened by the legislative process, and it could also be used to govern the marital issues of the LGBT community, which is an emerging issue in the present era's evolving society. Also, in the said act, registration of marriage under sections 15 and 16 is very lengthy and takes much time. The legislature should thus provide for a shorter period and a speedier process of registration. The issues related to inter-caste marriages often have families of both parties involved. In order to have a progressive stance towards the problem, it is also essential that the mediation mechanism be strengthened because such issues also have an emotional angle that needs to be addressed.

· **Findings**

Though the whole discussion lays down prospects for an upcoming society, this comes with several challenges too. During the writer's survey, it was found that in the village, there had been only five cases of widow remarriage, out of which four had been primarily to gain economic benefits from the widow's family. Furthermore, the caste-based and religion-based differences are still dominant on a large scale in their society.

The writer, in his confidential survey, also found out that the practice of dowry had been prevalent even in the cases of love marriage, where individuals had married by choice. The Panchayat has often tried to eliminate this practice from the village society but has been largely unsuccessful due to the lack of consensus among the village residents. Such practices often promote economic disparities due to the movement of resources in a large amount, from one section of society to the other, which might hamper the nation's progress.

Any system of cooperation exists when the interests of individuals are vested. Similar is the case with the institution of marriage, where individuals come together in order to satisfy their own needs physical, emotional, biological, social. Marriage has always been considered as an opportunity for the spiritual growth of a human being, and that is probably why in every ancient society, whatever be the religion, the institution of marriage has always existed, playing a dominant role in society and its people's lives. With the coming of western influence in the Indian society, the country has seen a rise in the cases of divorce, which can prove to be detrimental for Indian society in the present stage, when divisions are on a rise because in present conditions when society is getting divided, a division in its fundamental blocks would lead the society to fall apart.

· **Conclusion**

An issue often associated with the case of "love marriages "is that girls are generally in fear of being disowned by their families under societal pressure. This issue can be resolved by social reforms for the dilution of the institution of caste and by taking steps for the economic empowerment of women. Mediation, as discussed earlier, could also be a solution. In order to achieve the goals as outlined in the paper, it is necessary to bring cooperation from different fields of the society such as authorities, education. If we are, in future, able to reach a consensus and realize this goal in the form of a uniform civil code, then we would emerge as a strong nation. The result of this achievement would be that India would set an example for the whole world, and the Indian legal system could provide a framework for cooperation among the different sections and factions that exist in different parts of the world.

· **References**

1. Writ Petition (Civil) No. 231 of 2010
2. Criminal Appeal No. 366 of 2018 (Arising out of S.L.P. (Crl.) No. 5777 of 2017)
3. 2017 10 S.C.C. 1
4. Writ Petition (Civil) No. 231 OF 2010
5. Writ Petition (CRL) No. 955 of 2021
6. Gani, H. A. (1978). Muslim Political Issues and National Integration. Sterling Publishers, P.3
7. Portuguese Civil Code, 1867
8. The Constitution of India, 1950
9. The Hindu Marriage Act, 1955
10. The Special Marriage Act, 1954

VII
Domestic Violence Amidst Lockdown In India

Authored By: Abhinesh Soni

- **Abstract**

Covid-19 has severely impacted the world and has forced different countries affected by it to bitterly undergo either complete or partial lockdown in order to curb the threat. However, with the commencement of lockdown, particularly in India, severe challenges and unprecedented situations were faced across the length and breadth of the country. The country's people had faced gross infringement of fundamental human rights to food, clothing and travel. Nonetheless, with more and more people being forced to comply with the 'stay at home' restrictions, there has been an increase in gender-based violence testified by the World Health Organization. The efforts of various NGOs and other reports reflect the rise of domestic violence against women in India and across the world amidst the lockdown. Evident from the rise of domestic violence cases, home, ideally considered a safe place and only remedy against covid-19, had turned out to be perilous for women. Also notable from the National Commission for Women (NCW) Chairperson, Rekha Sharma's remarks, that the high number is attributable to the lockdown imposed as a result of the coronavirus outbreak, which had kept the abuser and victim together.

Nonetheless, domestic violence cases shall be estimated to be more than the reported number as the cases were reported mainly via emails and phones. Hence, a derivation can be drawn that only a section of women who had access to technology was mainly able to report the cases mentioned above during the lockdown. This essay scrutinizes domestic violence faced by women in India amidst lockdown and the lack of proper steps taken by the state in acknowledging and addressing the seriousness of the distress and its implications. This essay further institutes the need of maintaining social distance with misogynist ideas and practices existing in the society, in addition to physical distancing.

- **Keywords:***domestic violence, child, offences, covid19, WHO*

- **Introduction**

An unprecedented situation had forced several countries across the world to undergo lockdown in order to tackle the Covid-19 menace. As per The Economic Times, "A lockdown is an emergency protocol that prevents people from leaving a given area. A full lockdown will mean you must stay where you are and not exit or enter a building or the given area. This scenario usually allows for essential supplies, grocery stores, pharmacies and banks to continue to serve the people. All non-essential activities remain shut for the entire period."

It had also given rise to other evils, such as domestic violence and abuse against women. India is not an isolated victim of this problem, but the problem of domestic violence is faced by most countries around the globe. The laws meant to protect women fell short as women failed to reach the concerned authorities, and thus, this led to a subsequent increase in domestic violence cases in the country. The reason behind such atrocities was an accumulation of frustration and a shift from everyday routine life. Various measures were undertaken by the governments across the state and country and also internationally to curb this menace. The pandemic is a silent signal, indicating how our laws had not been able to fulfil their essential purpose of protecting women and thus, there stands a need to introduce urgent measures and rectify the existing laws to stop such atrocities.

- **Women and Violence**

Violence against women is a consequence of the old system of patriarchy. Various factors make it extremely difficult for women to leave violent households. Whether belonging to high or low strata of society, a woman's successful relationship with her family, especially her husband and in-laws, is used to validate her integrity; this societal pressure makes it hard for women to leave abusive partners and households. Due to poverty, lack of resources or even patriarchy, many women are left with insufficient or no skills to make an independent living, forcing them to be economically dependent on their husbands. Another reason why many women stay with their abusive partners is to protect their children. There are several instances of men being granted custody of their children even after showing abusive tendencies. Men who are abusive to their spouses and are likely to abuse their children as well. Many people had taken the pandemic as an opportunity to marry off minors, especially young girls, to older men. The cases of child marriages had increased radically due to the lockdown, which had led to parents of child brides marrying them off early; other reasons include the closing of schools, the weddings being less expensive due to lockdown restrictions and laidback monitoring and surveillance during the lockdown, making it easy and convenient to marry off young children secretly. As reported in The Times of India, near about 92,203interventions were made by CHILDLINE, which is a nodal agency working under the Ministry of Women and Child development to safeguard women in a troubling time of lockdown; out of total complaints, 35% were related to child marriage. Another report in The Times of India stated that in Latur, after her sister's death, a 15-year-old girl was the sacrificial bride on offer to a 50-year-old man. However, the marriage was timely intruded. Children trapped in abusive households often fall prey to emotional and physical trauma. Primarily due to the lockdown, children spend more time at home and are more exposed to mental health issues.

- **Laws against domestic violence in India**

Domestic violence is one of the most predominant problems in India, and Indian legislation to curb the same had introduced laws. Some of the most prominent laws are the

- **Dowry Prohibition Act 1961**

This is a criminal law and punishes taking or giving of dowry. Under this Act, if someone physically or mentally pressurizes shall be liable for imprisonment for six months or fined up to Rs. 5000.

- **498A of Indian Penal Code. (Criminal Amendment Act 1863)**

The third law that helps women who face violent behaviour at home is section 498A of IPC. This law applies to husbands who are harsh or cruel to women. Cruelty means any conduct that compels the woman to commit suicide or causes grave injury to her life. It also encompasses harassment in the name of dowry. If convicted, there is imprisonment of 3 years.

- **Domestic Violence Act 2005**

According to the preamble, this Act strengthens the constitutionally provided protection of women's rights, which are victims of domestic violence of any sort, as well as things related to or incidental to it. (Debalina Chatterjee, 2018). This law extends help to married women and any woman who was once in a domestic relationship and was subject to domestic violence. Also, this Act provides protection to children who are below 18 years and extends protection to the adopted, step or foster children. This Act allows the Magistrate to pass a protection order to ensure that the concerned woman does not contact the abuser. The abuser can be a husband or relatives of the husband, including men and women.

The procedure involved under the Act is tailor-made in order to safeguard the complete protection of women. Some of the critical sections are:

1.) The Act allows any person who believes that the Act of domestic violence has taken can report it to the Protection Officer (PO). (Section 4)

2.) Women under the Act shall be informed about their rights which includes making applications for obtaining remedy by way of a protection order or monetary relief, or any other order. (Sec 5)

3.) The (P.O.) makes a Domestic violence incidence report and then sends copies of it to the Police officer in charge (Sec 9). The Magistrate is required to fix a 1st date of hearing (Sec 12).

4.) The P.O. shall serve notice of hearing given by the Magistrate on the respondent and any other person as directed by the Magistrate. (Sec 13)

This particular Act, is a big step, in addition to prior legislations and gives this offence an expanded definition to the term domestic violence. Section 3 defines an act consisting of physical, emotional, mental, verbal and sexual abuse and includes harassment for the dowry. The Act also includes compensation from domestic abuse and encompasses maintenance in line with section 125 of CrPC. It is to be noted that maintenance allowed under this Act shall correspond with the lifestyle of the aggrieved party. This Act also provides support to the victims of domestic and emotional abuse. Also, the enactment of this Act was with recourse to Article 253 of the constitution, which confers power to parliament to make laws following international treaties. The Domestic Violence Act was passed after ratification by the U.N. Committee on the CEDAW.

- **Significant Impact of Laws**

Section 498A was introduced to protect women from the cruel behaviour of husbands and their relatives. The section protects women against mental and physical cruelty. This section was only limited to cruelty to married women, and all other forms of domestic violence were covered under individual acts of violence given under IPC and but in IPC, there was no measure to allow her to stay in the matrimonial house and suffer from other shortcomings, thus to cover these shortcomings were covered under The Domestic Violence Act of 2005. This law was introduced to uphold rights provided to women under Articles 14, 15 and 21 of the Constitution to save women. The Act provides a piece of effective machinery to ensure the protection of women.

Even after having these laws, in a pandemic, there was a surge of domestic violence cases in India. The sole reason why laws were incapable of resolving the issue is that there is a lack of awareness among people for the existing laws. In Section 11 of the Domestic Violence Act itself, the government must endorse and raise awareness in society by reaching out to people and through the use of print media, which does not adhere and is one of the reasons for the increase in domestic violence cases in the country. Also, the Act in section 7 requires

medical assistance to women, which is also not complied with. (Pooja Soni and Mitali Goyal 2020). No such awareness was undertaken by the government of India. Also, in India, marital laws have not been recognized as sexual offence and are considered a duty towards husband and thus, allows men to exert violence in the form of sexual violence and therefore, even when there is a destructive sexual relationship, it will not be considered as marital rape. Additionally, the laws failed to protect women because of the crippled form of communication in the lockdown. The contact number launched by NCW had limited reach, and women could not move out expressing their miseries. Thus, making this system a failure. (Kanika Arora and Shubham Kumar 2020). Often women who seek protection from abusive husbands are directed to live in shelter homes. However, often these shelter homes are overcrowded. Also, police who had to play an active role in ensuring women's safety mainly were deployed, ensuring that lockdown norms were maintained. If we read laws that are laid out for the protection of women, we come across the fact that there are many practical problems such as refusal by police to implement such laws and also low conviction under 498A in the criminal justice system.

· **Prevailing Violence during Covid-19**

In order to protect its citizens from the perils of lockdown, the government of respective nations completely locked their countries down. However, this decision was viewed as a prudent approach to tackle the coronavirus, but with this lockdown, women experienced real danger as there was a surge of domestic violence cases. As per WHO, one out of the three women globally experiences bodily or sexual offence by the perpetrator in their life span, and these obnoxious acts arise during any emergency and epidemic. (WHO 2020) Older women, women with disabilities or women living as refugees and living in conflicted regions are more prone to such atrocious acts. United Nations chief Antonio Guterres also called for steps to observe, "horrifying global surge in domestic violence" against women. (United Nation 2020). The domestic violence issue was prevalent worldwide, and many experts expressed it as "intimate terrorism". (Amanda Taub 2020)

Similarly, there had been an increase in domestic violence cases in countries, such as the United Kingdom, where website visits, calls, and emails received had increased manifold. Also, there had been murders of women and children reported in the first three weeks. In Australia, there was a 40 per cent increase, and in Argentina, there was an increase by 25 per cent. (Amanda Taub, 2020)

- ## Domestic Violence in India

In India, there was a substantial increase in domestic violence cases reported since lockdown started, with more husbands vent their anger on women. Within a few weeks of the lockdown, there was a substantial increase, as noted by the National Commission of Women (NCW). (ARJUN KUMAR, BALWANT SINGH MEHTA, and SIMI MEHTA, 2020). The NCW Chairperson, Rekha Sharma, further remarked that actual figures may be more than the ones reported as most of the complaints were via mail, or phones which is still not the preferred mode by most vulnerable women of India and also abused women may be prevented from using phones by violent perpetrators. Between March and April, there were more than 1000 complaints of violence against women. Being in lockdown with these violent perpetrators could lead to physical and sexual abuse and thus, can tarnish the mental stability of such women. Often women are forced into sexual intercourse, and thus, this calls for stringent law relating to marital rape.

National Legal Service Authority (NALSA) has collected data from the various legal service authorities about cases relating to domestic violence. NALSA, which reports to its executive chairman Justice N.V Sharma showed the increase in domestic violence cases in different states.

- ## Causes

The primary reason for domestic violence amidst the lockdown is the frustration of losing jobs and being bound by various constraints due to lockdown. This frustration takes the form of abuse on the women of the house. Most victims are unable to seek help due to the restriction of staying at home. The police are exhaustively occupied with ensuring strict implementation of the curfew, leaving the suffering women with lesser modes of seeking help and support.

1. The pandemic has led to a decrease in payment for some and loss of jobs for others owing to lockdown. This has caused loss of financial security for many families leading men to turn towards domestic abuse.

2. The worry of financial instability and insecurity of not being re-employed leads to stress and anxiety. Some perceive masculinity as being able to earn bread and butter; in these instances, when a job is threatened,

masculinity allegedly becomes vulnerable too.

3. Isolating oneself is new to most. The frustration of adhering to strict lockdown restrictions and being confined inside a limited space is one of the reasons.

4. Amidst stressful environments, many abusers have found solace in substance abuse. Alcohol and distress work synergistically. Alcohol is a depressant, and when it is consumed during suffering, it would only prove to elevate the misery in an abusive relationship. In one of the reported cases in Hyderabad, a woman and her son from a previous marriage faced abuse from her husband due to frustration of inability to access alcohol. Also, the first step taken by the government to ease lockdown was to open alcohol shops even in the most sensitive areas of lockdown, further aggravating the problem. (The Indian Express 2020). The cruelty of the violence faced by women amplified after the husband came to know that she had filed a complaint. (Shemin Joy, 2020).

5. Due to lockdown, women are trapped with their abusers and even if they wish to seek help from friends and family, it would not be possible. Also, the restricted movement does not allow them to get help from the police and organizations. Thus, the women who wish to free themselves from the abuse cannot do the same.

6. How the victims could get help were also limited during the lockdown. The limited means were phones and the internet. Some women do not have access to phones and technology, which limits them from receiving help.

7. The police had specific duties to ensure the smooth imposition of the lockdown, which makes them not adequately responsive to domestic violence complaints. There had been incidents where the police did not cooperate with punishing the abusers.

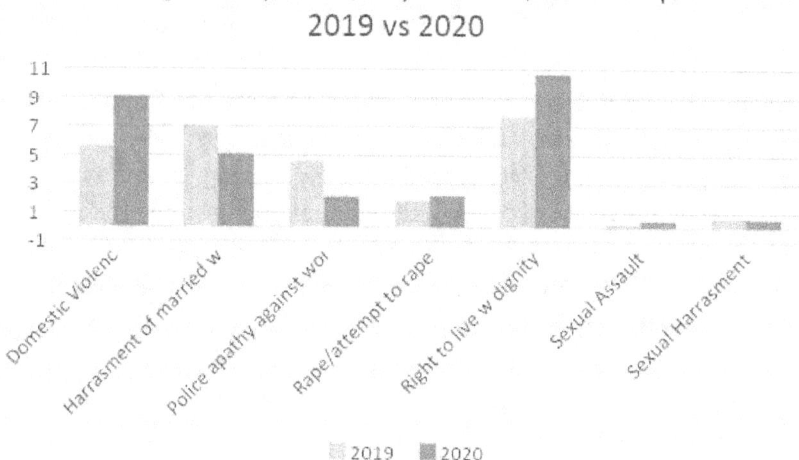

(Source: Ashwini Deshpande, In locked down India, women fight coronavirus and domestic violence, Quartz India, (April 16, 2020) available at: https://qz.com/india/1888351/indias-coronavirus-lockdown-leads-to-more-violence-against-women)

- **U.N. domestic violence reduction recommendations:**

- Recommendation of increasing investment in online services and civil societies.
- Ensuring prosecution of perpetrators of domestic violence.
- Setting up a warning and emergency mechanisms in pharmacies and groceries.
- Declaring shelters as an essential service.
- They are creating a safe passage for women to seek support.
- Avoiding parole and release of convicts of domestic violence.
- Increasing awareness and campaigns especially targeting men and boys.

- **Gaps in U.N. recommendation and government's response in India**

All over, the worldwide outpouring of domestic violence cases did attract sufficient coverage by both national as well as international media. Various countries took safety measures to curtail the problem. However, the Indian government failed to step out to fight domestic violence, which is a pandemic in disguise. Also, the U.N. recommendations were not implemented in the country widely as no advisory was issued nationally in India. The Prime Minister of the country addressed the nation regularly, but there was no mention of the rising domestic violence cases during the lockdown. No measures guaranteeing the safety of the vulnerable women and children were taken by the child and women ministry. There was no mention of helping women fromlower-income strata by launching or suggesting modes of filing complaints. Measures like the allotment of safe houses for the victims and their children were also not taken.

- **Initiatives and steps are taken to Curb Domestic Violence**

In order to curb domestic violence cases, few initiatives were taken that were praiseworthy. The department of Education's Mahila Samakya organized initiatives of Nari Adalat and Sahara Sangh in 2 districts of U.P and Gujarat. Also, Salishe, a traditional method, was being utilized by NGOs (Shramajibee Mahila Samiti). Also, to create more awareness and reach out to women at large, ICRW held television programs on four channels which were entitled "Bol", which created a positive effect on women.

Police in Uttar Pradesh, which had the worst track records on domestic violence cases in India, had launched a new helpline number for women affected.

The High Court of Delhi directed the Centre government and Delhi in the suit filed by NGO, in case of All India Council of Human Rights, Liberties and Social Justice (AICHILS) V. Union of India. Delhi High Court was reached by the NGO to hold- up a top-level meeting in order to take measures to curb the rising cases of domestic violence in the country amidst lockdown and protect the victims. In hearing of the case, the government of Delhi and Delhi Commission of Women (DCW) submitted before the Court that was sufficient safeguards to ensure the safety of the victims and children. (NDTV, 2020)

Also, the Jammu and Kashmir High court on a suo- moto notice concerning violence against women during the lockdown. The Court issued notices to the Jammu and Kashmir governments to give a detailed report of the safety measures and forms of violence faced by women amidst the lockdown. (Leaf Let, 2020)

- **Role of Non-State Actors in India**

In hard times when no one could move out of their houses, there were some significant initiatives taken for women by non-state actors, particularly NGOs who stood by to offer help and shelter to the victims of domestic violence.

Vishakha, an NGO in Rajasthan, was dedicated to supporting the working migrant women. Even though government machinery failed to serve the women around the country when the lockdown was announced, Vishakha continued working for deprived women. Understanding the dire need for sanitary napkins, contraceptives and emergency pills, the NGO addressed these necessary needs of the workers and women. (AATHIRA KONIKKARA, 2020) Similarly, Shakti Shalini, a Delhi based NGO, was running a 24-hour helpline to address the needs and issues of women. The NGO registered a stark increase in the number of calls made by women than what they used to receive before lockdown; also, the NGO pointed out that there could be more such victims, but since they live with abusers 24x7, it becomes difficult for them to reach out. (Dhamini Ratnam 2020) In Kolkata, an NGO named Swayam worked out to dispatch rations to women in need, and the NGO also maintained touch with women of the society who were facing domestic violence and needed support. The NGO also reported an increase in domestic violence complaints at the time of lockdown. (Print 2020) In Jharkhand, Association for Advocacy and Legal Initiatives ensured that the police registered cases and FIRs against abusive husbands and tried to reach out to women who had suffered violence (Neetu Singh, 2020). **Nazariya,** a Delhi-based organization that focuses on problems affecting lesbian, bisexual women, and trans people assigned female at birth, held weekly video-conferencing sessions. Zoom was used to compensate for the fact that in-person interactions with LGBT people who did not have a support system at home were impossible. (Dhamini Ratnam 2020). The work undertaken by the NGOs all over the country was a big help to women across the country.

- **Steps that should have been taken to protect atrocities against women in covid-19**

1. The initiatives undertaken at school are well placed to curb violence and offence against women. School centric programmes can address gender

norms and attitudes before it gets too late and is ingrained in the hearts of society's children. Such initiatives focus on gender norms, dealing with sexual abuse among teenagers and youth. Significant changes and positive reports have been reported for similar programmes named Safe Dates programme in USA and Youth relationship projects practised in Canada.

2. Women can be empowered, and men can be engaged through community actions. Gender norms and attitudes could be addressed in communities through a combination of microfinance for females and males—and methods that empower males as participants in the fight against gender-based violence. The most substantial proof is for the IMAGE microfinance and gender fairness initiative in South Africa and the stepping stones programme in Africa and Asia. Community programmes involving male peer groups can change attitudes about conventional gender norms and aggressive behaviour, but more thorough assessments are needed. The effectiveness of these interventions appears to be boosted by well-trained facilitators and community ownership.

3. It is essential to understand the role of media intervention; this intervention can change norms and advocate women's rights. Also, public awareness campaigns other such activities, which are delivered via T.V., radio and other print media and mass media, can be significant for changing perception and attitude towards women and gender norms. The most successful interventions seek to understand its target audience and engross with other members to develop more media content.

4. Also, it is to be noted that any initiative and programs shall engage both men and women. There are instances and proofs that microfinance schemes designed for empowering women (without involving males) may cause friction and conflicts between spouses, particularly in societies that follow rigid gender roles. Further, there is a need to explore how such possible adverse effects shall be overcome.

5. It is also necessary that policy interventions shall emphasize long-term goals of changing partisan social issues, eradicating gender gaps, whether they are educational, financial or economic. Also, the focus shall be on designing an aggressive and advanced policy that targets altering outcomes such as giving voice to women in the community.

6. The creation of national and state helplines in coordination with civil society was essential as there must be a dedicated hotline for victims of domestic violence in India, voluntary organizations which will receive complaints and coordinate with the concerned police station to ensure that

there is no misuse or abuse of power by the police.

· Conclusion

With the lifting of lockdown, the number of domestic violence cases might reduce, but the problem itself will not be solved as it is deeply rooted in the systematic oppression of women. The government had not only failed to tackle the rise in the cases mentioned above but also to acknowledge it. Although there are numerous legislations to guard women, their mere existence is not sufficient for the protection of women. Particular policies are required to be made and implemented in emergencies such as a pandemic.

· References

1. THE DOWRY PROHIBITION ACT, 1961, India (28 of 1961).
2. THE CRIMINAL LAW (SECOND AMENDMENT) ACT, Sec 498A. (46 OF 1983).
3. Kanika Arora and Shubham Kumar 2020, Locked-down: Domestic Violence Reporting in India during covid19, https://www.oxfamindia.org/blog/locked-down-domestic-violence-reporting-india-during-covid-19.
4. United Nation (2020) U.N. chief calls for domestic violence 'ceasefire' amid 'horrifying global surge', https://news.un.org/en/story/2020/04/1061052.
5. Amanda Taub (2020) A New Covid-19 Crisis: Domestic Abuse Rises Worldwide, THE INTERPRETER.
6. ARJUN KUMAR, BALWANT SINGH MEHTA, SIMI MEHTA, (2020) The link between lockdown, COVID-19, and domestic violence.
7. PB, Mehta (2020) We need to question our addiction to the cultural and political economy of alcohol.